WHERE EARTH MEETS HEAVEN
Seeing God in Your Life

KEN ROLHEISER

ST. ANTHONY MESSENGER PRESS
Cincinnati, Ohio

Scripture citations are taken from *New Revised Standard Version Bible*, copyright ©1989 by the Division of Christian Education of the National Council of the Churches of Christ in the U.S.A., and used by permission. All rights reserved.

Cover and book design by Mark Sullivan

Library of Congress Cataloging-in-Publication Data

Rolheiser, Kenneth.
  Where Earth meets heaven : seeing God in your life / Kenneth Rolheiser.
    p. cm.
  ISBN 0-86716-578-2 (alk. paper)
  1. Spiritual life—Catholic Church. I. Title.
  BX2350.3.R65 2004
  248.4'82—dc22
                                        2003025702

ISBN 0-86716-578-2

Published by St. Anthony Messenger Press
www.AmericanCatholic.org
Printed in the U.S.A.

I dedicate this book to my family,
God's loving touch and sparkling presence in my life.

contents

foreword

My life has had many blessings. One of these is the grace of having grown up with seven brothers. Among those, I am closest in age to my brother Ken, two years my senior, the author of this book. Being that close to each other in age meant we went through our boyhood and school years sharing, conscriptively and voluntarily, a lot of things—clothes, a bedroom, friends, classrooms, reactions to world events, experiences of every kind.

I always looked up to him, and with reason. He was older, taller, more handsome, more athletic, more popular, more self-assured, more articulate and more mature. But he didn't lord that over me. He was always solicitous for my welfare and, not infrequently, bailed me out when I made mistakes and was too immature to face the consequences. Not that it was all romantic. We fought, too—the usual sibling stuff—and today we recall with humor many such incidents, including one where we got into some childish spat while hauling grain from a combine and I swung first, bloodied his nose, and then ran home across a grain field for a mile or so. He could, of course, have caught me and retaliated. He didn't. That wasn't his style, then or now.

The incidents of rivalry were minor and infrequent. Mostly he was a wonderful brother and I stood in admiration of him, even if I stood somewhat in his shadow. That admiration hasn't diminished through the years, but increased.

When we graduated from high school, the rite of passage for leaving home in our family, we went our separate ways and on to separate lives. He went on to marriage—a wonderful one—to a teaching career, to becoming the father of four talented, beautiful children, and to years of service in both his civic and church community. I went on to the seminary, to priesthood, and to duties that kept taking me further and further away from home. But we kept in touch through the distance and the years. I've watched his children grow up and he (with no gray hair, despite being my senior) watched my hair grow thin and gray. He still stands taller, my older brother in every way.

Today we write from our separate experiences—he from his experience of marriage, raising a family, teaching high school, being involved with civic and church community, and wanting more and more to touch and drink from his roots: faith, family, and geography. I write from my experience of celibacy, of priesthood, of being a missionary, of being privileged enough to sit in some first-rate graduate schools, and of working with so many both happy and wounded people in ministry. We write from different perspectives, but our common background reveals itself in our writings. We're brothers—and it shows.

Our souls were very much shaped by the same forces, the same parents, family life, moral background, and spiritual geography. I mention this last element because nobody who was born and raised in those lonely, over-spacious, mosquito-ridden, drought-prone, merciless, wonderful, North American prairies isn't significantly shaped by them. They have a beauty all their own, the kind that invites you to be humble and resilient, both at the same time, and that shapes you to be a football fan, to watch the weather for rain or drought, to not take yourself too seriously, to see everyone as your neighbor, to be self-deprecating because you come from the prairies, to be robust because that's what it takes to survive out there, and to notice the space and providence that God provides in such abundance. Ken shapes his words from this perspective.

What you read in this book, *Where Earth Meets Heaven,* is my brother's experience of marriage, family life, parenting, teaching, local community and universal church life, all set into that special spiritual geography that so much shaped his soul, my own, and those of our contemporaries. These essays wonderfully reflect my brother—his transparency, his faith, his dedication to family, church, community, his love for his roots, his steady moral compass, his eye for prairie beauty and his maturity.

The title is appropriate, a hermeneutical key to understanding both the essays and their author. *Where Earth Meets Heaven* describes my brother's ground experience of life, namely, that underneath everything else, no matter how cloudy the day or dark the horizon, we're still safe because we're in more safe, more loving and more gentle hands than our own.

Ron Rolheiser
ROME, ITALY
SEPTEMBER 21, 2003

Introduction

The people who walked in darkness
  have seen a great light;
those who lived in a land of deep darkness—
  on them light has shined. (Isaiah 9:2–4)

This book is about Good News. It is about being at the place where earth meets heaven, the place where we live our daily lives. This is where we meet or miss meeting Jesus; it is where those around us can meet Jesus through us.

Seeing the world in spiritual terms is not the reserve of monks, nuns and ordained clergy. "Mysticism is in fact a very ordinary experience, an experience open to all and had by all. Simply defined, mysticism is being touched by God..."[i] in a way we cannot think, express, picture or clearly feel. "Everyone is touched, held, and seared by God ...unless one lacks purity of heart...is hardened by sin..."[ii] If one lives in purity of heart, then God will color that person's heart, life and perception. *Where Earth Meets Heaven* explores the theme of spirituality for the layperson. It is written by a layperson and for laypeople. This book is an answer to a spiritual hunger in the souls of many, including many who have abandoned institutional religion.

Where Earth Meets Heaven touches upon the countless ways we experience God's love in our daily lives. It reaches out with hope and humor to bring light into a world that is often too gloomy. Karl Rahner in *Prayer for a Lifetime* says, "Most of the time when we sin, we do know what we are doing, but we don't know how much God loves us—hence we are still innocent through ignorance." This book is about our innocence—the innocence redeemed by Christ's loving sacrifice. It is ultimately a book of hope.

This book was exciting to write. The ideas sprang from several years of writing a spiritual column for secular weekly newspapers in which I attempted to reach the widest audience. I knew I was on the right track when a young man—a man who had stopped attending church services on Sundays—said that he enjoyed reading the articles. The response from many of my readers has inspired me, and their prayers have helped to keep me on the right path.

I wish also to acknowledge the influence of another author and gifted spiritual writer, my younger brother Ron Rolheiser. Ron's writings have influenced my life and my writing. In my articles I often quote from his works, because no one says it better. His many illustrations have influenced my literary style, and his personal example has inspired my life.

NOTES

[i] Here I quote and paraphrase from Ronald Rolheiser's *The Shattered Lantern* (New York: Crossroad, 2001), p. 67

[ii] Rolheiser, *Shattered Lantern*, p. 68.

CHAPTER ONE

Jesus in Our Daily Lives

WHERE EARTH MEETS HEAVEN

There is a story told about ancient monks who searched the earth looking for the door to heaven. Finally, they stood at the threshold of the place where earth meets heaven. When they opened the door, they were back at their monastery, where they lived their daily lives.

Mysticism, our union with Christ, is God's desire. Jesus wants us to grow so close to him that it goes beyond all human bonds. So close that when our moment of death arrives we can simply put ourselves into the hands of our savior and stop worrying. So close that when others look at us, they see more than us; they see Jesus himself.

When infants look at their parents, they see someone who is more than human. They see someone who knows all the mysteries of life, someone who understands the world of darkness and death, someone who is like Jesus. This is a humbling experience for parents.

I had a similar experience when I visited my older sister, an Ursuline nun, who was dying of cancer. Sister Helen was in and out of consciousness, a mere shell of her former self. I was taken aback because she seemed to grow alert and say, "You are here? I'm so sorry!" I was shocked that, despite her pain and condition, she should worry about the long drive I had made to see her—some three hundred kilometers on winter roads. I could not believe it! "I'm sorry," she repeated.

"It's all right," I assured her. "It's all right." I continued to assure her.

Later, in one of her lucid moments, she told one of my sisters that she had seen Jesus. Sister Helen was happy and could peacefully face death because Jesus had told her it was all right.

The greatest role that you and I can play in God's kingdom on earth is to be at the place where earth meets heaven. It is a simple goal to achieve: a kind word, a drink of water, a visit to a shut-in, a smile! "Inasmuch as you have done this to the least of my brethren, you have done it to me!"

When I was a child, my family celebrated Christmas Eve with a German tradition of the Christ Child. It was tremendously popular with the younger children. In anticipation of Jesus' visit, we would be on our best behavior all through Advent. Often at sunset we would notice the glow in the sky and say that the Christ Child was baking Christmas cookies. And no matter how cold it got, there was always one little corner of the window that had no frost on it—that's where Jesus was watching us to see if we were good, we'd tell one another.

When the afternoon light faded on the farm and the chores were done, supper was a blur of excitement. The "schnitz soup" warmed excited children and adults gathered round the table. As soon as the dishes were done, everyone quickly donned their Sunday best to wait for the Christ Child to arrive. Usually, once we heard that long-awaited knock on the front door, one of the older brothers or sisters would answer the door and go outside to tether the donkey while the Christ Child entered. We saw a figure in dazzling white, with a branch in his hand. On the branch was a white ribbon. The Christ Child was really here! He asked questions of us children. "Were you good?" "Did you obey your parents?" I was always too breathless to answer. He brought a box of gifts for everyone.

In later years, I had to overcome the bitter disappointment I suffered when I discovered the "Christ Child" was actually my brother one year, my sister another. Then it was my turn to participate in "the game" myself—helping to move the gifts out an upstairs window to a nearby granary. Ultimately, however, I came to understand a great truth: When we do see Christ, we see him in each other. I *had* seen Christ when I was a child. Even with her homemade lye soap, Mom

4

could never have gotten the garment as white and dazzling as what I saw with eyes of faith on that Christmas Eve.

Just recently, I got to see Jesus again—touching people, walking among them, shaking their hands and comforting them. Our group was performing some scenes from *The Mystery of the Passion of Christ* at a senior home. As I watched the soldiers mistreat Christ, I observed one senior, in particular, weeping and quite distraught—not an unusual reaction in our audiences. After the performance, Peter Champagne, the actor who played Christ, was moved to go from senior to senior, shaking a hand, touching a brow, comforting with a word.

Peter later observed to me that some of the seniors thought he was really Jesus. I assured him that, in fact, he *was* Jesus to them. As members of the cast of *The Mystery of the Passion of Christ* we have become aware, over time, that we are part of a deeper mystery that touches on the drama of real lives. We are aware and grateful for others who have worked hard planting the seed of faith that is stirred by our performance. Perhaps those in our audience were formed in the faith by their parents, perhaps by a catechist or a minister, but all were led by that faith to this performance, where hearts are touched, spiritual longings are stirred, and in the end, "sower and reaper rejoice together."

The leap of faith is not a large one here. Our role as Christians is to be Christ to one another. As we do this, we are not always aware of how real our role is in life's drama. To be mistaken for Christ is the highest compliment, but it is no more than doing what is our duty. In John 4:37–38 Jesus describes the harvest of this world and our role: " 'One sows and another reaps.' I sent you to reap that for which you did not labor. Others have labored, and you have entered into their labor."

Jesus is as close to us as our everyday experiences. That is where we find him or miss him. Ah! To be a Christian! To look at the world around us with the eyes of Christ! What a wonderful world it would be!

Recently I was seated in a throng of people watching a musical. I pondered what it would be like a thousand years in the future. Suddenly my discomforts and worries of the present seemed insignificant.

Suddenly all the people around me looked like friends—people I could love. If we had the vision of Christ and could see the present moment and its significance for all eternity, what a difference it would make! There would be no need for war; there would be no enemies. There would be no selfishness. Truly we would be ready to serve those around us. We would try to touch their hearts and not their pocket books. We would in fact be ready for Judgment Day.

In Matthew 25:34–36 Jesus gives us the vision we need to direct ourselves in this world. All that is truly important is given in this passage:

> Come, you that are blessed by my Father, inherit the kingdom prepared for you from the foundation of the world; for I was hungry and you gave me food, I was thirsty and you gave me something to drink, I was a stranger and you welcomed me, I was naked and you gave me clothing, I was sick and you took care of me, I was in prison and you visited me.

Nor should we neglect the spiritual works of mercy in our lives: instructing the ignorant, counseling the doubtful, comforting the sorrowful, bearing wrongs patiently, forgiving all injuries and praying for the living and the dead.

What a spectacular vision that final Judgment Day presents! Jesus smiling at us and welcoming us to the Father's kingdom. And why not? The Father has blessed us! Before the world was formed, he had us in his mind. He caressed us in our mother's womb. He sent his son to save us, to redeem our sins and to show us the way. It is so easy to see with the eyes of Christ. Look at those around you. See the sick or imprisoned and visit them. See the hungry. Break your bread and share. Share your extra cloak! Welcome the stranger. Keep an open heart! Do whatever you think God is leading you to do. The only thing that counts is the love with which you do it.

To be Jesus to others is simply to do what Jesus taught us to do. To be Christ to others is to do what Jesus would do, to be a disciple who ministers to others. In a real sense Jesus is in us. In the long discourse before his death he says to his disciples, to us: "On that day [after his Resurrection] you will know that I am in my Father, and you in me, and I in you" (John 14:20). And later in John 17:23 he says to the Father: "I in them [his disciples] and you in me, that they become completely one, so that the world may know that you have sent me..."

In this world where hatred lives and violence frequently explodes, we need to be peacemakers like Christ. We need to challenge social injustices. We need to visit shut-ins. We need the good will of the millions who responded to the charitable needs of the September 11 destruction. We also need to go on quietly supporting the charities that are not front-page news. And we need to continue quietly working and praying in a world where hatred frequently seems to thrive.

DAILY SPIRITUALITY

The challenge is to live our daily lives so that the simple, mundane activities of our existence become a significant part of our journey to the Father, even on days when it is hard to see that connection. Take for example the day they executed Timothy McVeigh, the Oklahoma City bomber. While this was happening, health-care workers in Saskatchewan were on strike, and I spent the day assisting twelve-hour nurses and struggling volunteers to bring care to seniors in a nursing home.

Let's look at these events one at a time. If Jesus Christ were being executed today, next to the Oklahoma bomber, he would go to his death much as he did two thousand years ago. He did not protest then, hanging between two thieves. He did not say, "Hey, I'm innocent! I'm not one of them!" He died for those thieves and made them one with him. Christ was beside McVeigh that morning. Christ's sacrifice and death were an eternal action to redeem sinners. Did the justice system have it right two thousand years ago? Did they have it right on this morning?

Seeing Christ in our fellow human beings is being spiritual. As I walked to the care home that morning, I thought of the messy diapers that needed changing. I thought of the ill and the incapacitated. It was time to act as a Christian, not just to keep an antiseptic distance. It was not easy to go to work as a Christian that morning, but I am glad that I did. I saw devoted volunteers working long hours—for some it was the third day. Cheerfully they cared for the patients in the endless cycle of feeding, changing, cleaning and attending to their every need. Some patients were ill; some were dying (in fact, I passed the undertaker wheeling out a body as I was taking a patient to breakfast). Some could not hear or see. But all were appreciative.

I thought of Mother Teresa's secret about tending the dying in the streets of Calcutta: "I am tending the body of Christ," she said. Seeing the Body of Christ in a fellow human being makes it possible to give that type of deep and devoted care.

Daily spirituality can be demanding at times. I left the care home that afternoon and it took me some time to recover my perspective. It was only later that I phoned back to an overworked administrator and volunteered my services for what turned out to be the next three days. The words of Saint James were haunting me and blessing me: "Charity without works is dead."

How do you experience God in your workaday world? Do you have to "screw up" your courage to face Monday morning? If you are interested in the answers to these questions you are on a spiritual journey. The experience of God is not only for recognized mystics. God is as close as our everyday work. Life can be deeply satisfying once we have some basic realizations—so basic that we need to remind ourselves of them occasionally or we will forget them.

Thomas Merton wrote:

> It is enough to be, in the ordinary human mode, with one's hunger and sleep, one's cold and warmth, rising and going to bed. Putting on blankets and taking them off, making coffee and drinking it. Defrosting the refrigerator, reading, meditating, working, and praying. I live as my fathers have lived on this earth; eventually I die. Amen.

There is a quiet dignity to our everyday tasks. These are simple things our parents and grandparents did before us. And this was part of the fabric of their lives, of their salvation.

I can vividly recall a hot July day I spent in simple tasks helping my wife in picking, preparing and canning vegetables. I was aware of patience and dignity in the work. The mosquito bites, the itch from the beans, tomatoes and cucumbers, not to mention the backache of stooping, attested to the metaphysical realities involved. This was a real life experience, not a cerebral exercise. With a small leap of faith, we can experience God in a way that is as tangible and as physical as this.

We humble creatures can become intimate with and close to our God and Creator. First we need to realize that God is there, all around us, as close as the air we breathe. His breath gives us life. He breathed life into our mud at creation. Without his love in creation, even for a second, the universe would crumble. It is only the power of the creator that sustains the universe and all its mighty forces.

There is a story about this in *The Shattered Lantern* by Ron Rolheiser:

> Imagine you are the mother fish and your child comes to you and says: "Mummy, where is this water we hear so much about?" Suppose, since this is a parable and anything is possible, you could do this. To give your child some sense of water, even though it is totally immersed within it, you could set up at the bottom of the ocean a slide projector and a television set and show your child pictures, slides and videos of water. As ironic as it would be, these pictures, which are not water, would in fact give your child, who is living in water, some idea of what water is. Eventually, after having shown your child hours of pictures of water, you might then want to turn off all the videos and the slide projector and simply tell the child: "Now you have some idea of what water is; you've seen pictures of it. Now I want you simply to sit in it and let it flow through you." That image, in essence, shows what meditation and contemplation of God are.[i]

Like the water surrounding the baby fish, giving it life, God's love surrounds us and gives us our very breath.

The secret to a closer relationship with our God is to sometimes sit, like Mary at the feet of Jesus, in silent meditation, contemplating God's presence, breathing in his gift of breath and asking ourselves: "Where is this water we hear so much about?"

Another way to be in touch with God on a daily basis is as simple as recalling the Lord's Prayer and reflecting on "Our Daily Bread" and its deeper spiritual implications. There is a story about an advertising genius who went to Budweiser and proposed that they try to change the words of the Lord's Prayer to get Christians around the world to say "Give us this day our daily beer." The brewery company thought this was great and went to the local bishop, who in turn went to a cardinal, who went to the Vatican. The Pope heard the plan and the huge sum Budweiser was prepared to pay. He thought of all the good that could be done with that money—the sick that could be cared for, the homeless that could be sheltered, the hungry that could be fed. He called a meeting of his top advisors to discuss the proposal. Turning to his financial secretary, he asked, "How much money are the folks at Wonder Bread paying us?"

What do we mean when we say, "Give us this day our daily bread"? Taking it literally, we think of food for our tables. But there is a much deeper spiritual implication. Christ called himself the "bread of life" (John 6:35), the bread that comes down from heaven. How great it would be to partake of that bread on a daily basis! The "bread of life" is good news for us. Jesus said whoever eats this bread will have life everlasting and will be raised up on the last day. In John 6:51 Jesus says: "I am the living bread that came down from heaven. Whoever eats of this bread will live forever." This was a difficult concept for Jesus' followers to accept. In John 6 Jesus says several times and in different ways: "Very truly, I tell you…those who eat my flesh and drink my blood abide in me and I in them." Jesus teaches in this passage that it is the Spirit that gives life. Just as Christ draws his life from the Father, so we can draw our life from Jesus (John 6:57–58). This is the "daily bread" we need to hunger for.

How often do we pray, "Give us this day our daily bread"? What does it mean? Do we have a daily connection with the "bread of life"? According to Jesus we do. In John 15:9 Jesus says, "As the Father has loved me, so I have loved you." The Father loved Jesus day by day. He followed him through his life's journey from his conception, to the flight into Egypt, to the outpouring of love on the cross. Now we are the children of God, in the family of God. And daily the Father looks on us with love as we journey through life.

The early church fathers used an analogy to express how God would ultimately assimilate us. In the natural order plants absorb minerals and animals eat plants. As we eat our daily food of plant or animal, our bodies are sustained. But this natural food is limited to our physical strength. The Eucharist or the Bread of Life is food of a higher order. It can nourish and sustain us with the life of Christ. We have Christ's word on the matter: "I am the bread of life." Within us we have the spark of the divine. As we grow spiritually by means of our daily communion with God (reading the Word in Scripture or partaking of the Eucharist), the "minerals" of our existence are transformed, in the supernatural order, into strength and health that is infinite and not limited to the physical plane.

Jesus said, "…whoever eats me will live because of me" (John 6:57). In the natural order there is no energy or power to bring us back to life after we die. In the higher order, the spiritual food of Jesus gives us life that will last beyond the physical. As we eat this daily bread his thoughts become our thoughts; his desires, our desires; and his life in us becomes our life, and can burn away all that is not holy. This is a lifelong process. It is worth pondering. If every time we pray "Give us this day our daily bread" we think about its profoundest meaning, our lives will be on a proper course. The Spirit will give us life that lasts forever!

DAILY WORK

Daily life to most of us involves hard work, which is often not soul-animating. Are you a saint where you live and work? There is a story about a Mafia figure who died. His brother came to see the priest and said, "I'll give you a half-million dollars for your parish fund if you stand up at the funeral tomorrow and say that my brother was a saint." "All right," the priest agreed. The next day he stood up at the funeral and said, "Today we are burying a man who was a criminal. He stole, he cheated, he lied and he had people killed. But compared to his brother, he was a saint."

All of us have a spark of God in us. What we do with that divine spark is our spirituality. In his book, *Spirituality @ Work: 10 Ways to Balance your Life and your Job*, Gregory Pierce says that God is in the noise, crowds and complexities of life. We do not find him only in retreats and solitude. Pierce says all spiritualities are based on practice. Saint James agrees: "Charity without works is dead" (James 2:17). Simply, the works we do in the spirit of Christ make us spiritual.

We find God in all the ordinary moments that make up our existence. I will briefly list ten examples of how I/we experience spirituality at work in our daily lives:

When I was a boy and my cousin was killed in a tractor accident, my older sister's reaction when she heard about it was to call on God: "O my God!"

When as a youth I saw a rosary hanging on my brother's farm tractor, and I knew that it was a natural part of his day on the field to recite that prayer;

When I was doing the most difficult task, like picking stones on the farm or cleaning a chicken barn on a hot day and I was sure I could feel the lice crawling on my neck, and I offered it as a prayer of atonement;

When I am turning from sin, realizing in the half-hearted gesture that my pride is still rationalizing—but God, like the Father in the Prodigal Son story, is stretching out his arms to me;

When I see the clouds playing over the rising sun, creating an extraordinary effect that tells me this is a special moment of grace;

When I find a moment of rest during a hectic day and make the sign of the cross and say "Thank you, God;"

When we gather as a community on Sunday morning, and it is a special day because I see so many present who do not always attend, especially the young;

When I held my firstborn child in my hands and saw the miracle that came about as a result of God blessing the love between my wife and me;

When I narrowly escape a collision on the highway or a fender-bender in town and say, "Thank you, Dad;"

When I tend the garden in summer and eliminate the weeds, like we do when we strive for order and justice in the workaday world of God's Kingdom and know that if God calls us home that night, our souls will be at peace and our Kingdom in order.

"If there are any wise or learned among you, let them show it by their good lives, with humility and wisdom in their actions" (James 3:13). Spirituality is walking with God daily and working for a world that has justice, generosity, integrity and loyalty. The real challenge is to translate this vision into the mire of everyday work. What is the ugliest job you ever had to do? For me, growing up on a farm, it was probably cleaning the chicken barn. A close second was spraying the chicken roosts for lice. Awful jobs, with nary a trace of salvation in them. Or was there? Odd as it may seem, the ugliest jobs and those that cause you the most pain are the ones that can get you to heaven. The trick is not to waste the opportunity.

My training in Catholic theology encouraged me to offer up all the work I do during the week. At Sunday morning Mass this work was united to the sacrifice of Christ who offered his very life for us. Work is a form of prayer. Believe me, when you stand in the stench of the chicken barn you consider the options. I have never wanted to waste this real experience of suffering. Work is prayer and can be offered up for our salvation or for some other intention. Not only the discomfort of work, but also every joyful, lawful activity can be offered up in the spirit of prayer.

One Thursday night, which was "movie night" in our rural parish of Saint Donatus, my mother was suffering a terrible gallstone attack. She was in real agony. The family decision was that we (the children) should go to the movie anyway, though it seemed to spoil the evening for us. I decided to simply offer up all the enjoyment and distraction the movie would afford, and offer this up for my mom's health. In retrospect, that was an excellent prayer. Not only did my mother's condition improve, but I was brought closer to understanding salvation. Everyday activities are how we relate to spiritual reality. Our everyday tasks are the opportunities presented to us through which we advance or miss our salvation. We only get to live this lifetime once.

HOLIDAY JOY

God made the earth and rested on the seventh day. The church encourages us to rest from our labors at least one day a week. Everyone loves a holiday, a time of no work, a time of pleasure, a time of recreation. There is a universal hunger for this sense of well-being, physical soundness and good health. Some of my colleagues teased me that I was doomed when I retired from teaching, because then I could never go on a holiday again. Happily, they were wrong. Writing keeps me busy enough to enjoy the occasional break.

I remember once trying to write an article on "holidays." In my enthusiasm to write the ultimate article on the theme of summer joy I checked the Internet under "holiday humor." I was quickly brought down to earth. I found a "blues" catalogue; I found a brief reference to an obituary about someone who apparently once had had a sense of humor, and I also found a German text which I quickly translated: "Are you looking for laughs, love, life? Then you are at the right place. Have you laughed yet today? If not, then just look once…into the mirror."

I grew up on a subsistence farm (we raised our meat, milk and eggs) and of necessity had a strong work ethic. "Idleness is the devil's workshop," my parents would recite and, believe me, they didn't want to give the devil a chance at us. Sunday was a holiday, really a "holy day" as its original meaning intended. And on that rare weekday that was deemed a holiday, great joy was experienced by all. Even now, in moments of deep meditation, when I want to recall a childhood memory of joy to restore my soul, I can put myself into a scene of holiday joy.

Workaholics experience guilt at the thought of taking off time to holiday. The need for recreation is just that, a need to re-create, to build anew our mental, physical and psychic energies. To look for a "spiritual" experience is attractive to most, but many are deterred by the word "religious." I recall the reaction of the editor of a weekly paper when I queried about publishing my articles in his paper: "[U]nlikely if religious..." The hesitation here is that "religion" normally implies a belief system that encompasses worship and the church. Spirituality, on the other hand, is an attractive term that depicts a universal hunger for some inner grace. It has to do with soul and spirit, which nobody wants to be without. If you pardon the analogy, it would be worse than admitting to being without a sense of humor.

There is a school of thought that suggests that if you find a job that you like, you will not have to work one day in your life—every day will be a holiday. I might add to this saying, "When we learn that work can be a prayer, every day of our lives will be a holy day."

NOTES

i Rolheiser, *The Shattered Lantern*, pp. 198-199.

CHAPTER TWO

Life's Paths

A philosophy professor stood before his class and began his experiment. First he took a mayonnaise jar and proceeded to fill it with rocks that were about two inches in diameter. Then he asked the students if the jar was full. They agreed that it was, so he picked up a box of pebbles and poured them into the jar. He shook the jar lightly. The pebbles, of course, rolled into the open areas between the rocks. The students laughed but couldn't see where he was going. The professor then picked up a box of sand and poured it into the jar. Of course the sand filled everything else.

"Now," said the professor, "I want you to recognize that this is your life. The rocks are the important things—your family, your partner, your children, your health—anything that is so important that if it were lost, you would be nearly destroyed. The pebbles are the other things that matter, like your job, your house, your car. The sand is everything else—the small stuff."

The professor looked at the students and made this application: "If you put the sand into the jar first, there is no room for the pebbles or rocks. The same goes for your life. If you spend all your energy and time on the small stuff, you will never have room for the things that are important to you. Pay attention to the things that are critical to your happiness. Play with your children. Take your partner out for dinner. Take time to have medical checkups. There will always be time to go to work, clean the house, give a dinner party and fix the disposable. Take care of the rocks first—the things that really matter. Set your priorities. The rest is just sand."[i]

We need to make room in our lives for the rock of our salvation. That is the "matter" that is eternal in us. Our dust will eventually return to the seashore as so much sand, but God's life in us, without which we really can't have a full life, is critical to our happiness, our fulfillment. We need to put God into our lives first, before it is too full of the small stuff. It is a matter of priorities.

God gives us the gift of time. We generally have years in which to grow out of our childhood, years of training for adult roles, and years to get involved in the busy aspects of our world. Somewhere, if we are not careful, the world takes over. We run out of hours in the day. Stop the music! Have a quiet hour. Revel in the 3600 seconds of an hour. Be a radical! Go for 7200! Time is a gift from God we need to reclaim. Will the world suffer if we miss one sports event, one episode of our favorite soap, one movie, (do I dare say it) one meeting? Take a break from the national news once. In that hour of silence, listen to the heart. Reflect on creation. Say "Thank you God." Reflect on the gift of time. Once you are refreshed, go back to the routine with a new understanding, a new presence as a participant. You are in control. Most people work eight hours and sleep eight hours. That still leaves eight hours over which we exercise some control. It seems hard to believe at times, but there really are twenty-four hours in a day.

I remember taking my own advice on this topic one Saturday, by avoiding an all-day, out-of-town meeting. I worked hard most of the day, using the gift of time I had taken back. I eased my conscience by reminding myself that I was just surviving in terms of meeting other obligations for the week. I could have gone to the meeting and handled the stress of overload. But I didn't. Time is a gift that God gives to each of us. None of us knows just how much time we have—all the more reason to cherish each moment and spend it wisely.

GOOD NEWS

> How beautiful upon the mountains
> are the feet of the messenger who announces peace,
> who brings good news. (Isaiah 52:7)

The world is crying out to hear Good News! Our everyday world feeds us enough disappointment, deception and despair to disillusion most.

Check the political campaigns. Is there hope and good news? Check the nightly news. By now this paragraph is almost an obstacle to the message I set out to express—good news. How easily we can get mired in the mud. If we are not careful, we can become an obstacle to the message of joy and hope that Christ wants us to impart to others.

Our life's journey should be one we take with light hearts. In Isaiah 52 we read about how happy our feet are as we bring the Good News. We should shout for joy rather than languish in sin and sorrow. Mark 10 tells the story of Bartimaeus, a blind beggar who shouts to attract the attention of Jesus, who is passing by. Many in the crowd around him, all for the best reasons, try "sternly" to shut him up so as not to disturb such a holy man or disrupt his journey. Jesus, knowing the situation, calls for Bartimaeus and cures him for his deep faith and for his courage in calling for help.

We are likely to be more like the bystanders in this story. We are relatively well-off, most of us—enough so that we have the resources and the leisure time to be reading. Sometimes we might inadvertently get in the way of God's work, even when we think we are doing God's will. We are afraid of scandal, concerned with appearances. An example from Morley Callaghan's novel, *Such Is My Beloved,* illustrates the point. A young priest is seen visiting the hotel rooms of prostitutes. He actually prays for the girls and gives them money to try to get them off the streets. But the well-meaning parishioners go to the bishop, who is also afraid that the scandal might affect his charity drive. I seriously wonder how we would react to such an apparently scandalous scene if it happened in our town.

In recent years we have witnessed the damage done by the church hierarchy when it seemed to be more concerned about stemming the spread of scandal than the prosecution of the guilty. We are not called to whitewash the church walls, or even our own outward appearance. We must proclaim the good news in our own lives and actions. We must be open to the Holy Spirit moving in our world, admit mistakes when we make them and celebrate the chance for repentance and grace.

IN THE BEGINNING

In Psalm 139:12–15 we read about how the creator knew us before we were born:

> For it was you who formed my inward parts;
> you knit me together in my mother's womb.
> I praise you, for I am fearfully and wonderfully made.

I always find this passage reassuring. God knew us before we were born. And God watches over us:

> You hem me in, behind and before,
> and lay your hand upon me. (Psalm 139:5–6)

Whatever path we walk, the loving hand of the Creator is there to guide us. And we have the assurance and protection of a God who loved us and knew us in the secret of darkness, before we saw the light, in our mother's wombs.

I had a dream one night that a small-town newspaper in Saskatchewan sent me a letter saying, "You should be in a better place." It took me a moment to realize that this was a great compliment. It implied I should be in a place like Saskatoon, Toronto or New York, where I imagine famous writers live. After waking I was led to a deeper reflection. We all should be in a better place. At Christmas we see an image of the crèche where the lamb lies down with the lion, where there is peace, and where Israelis and Palestinians, Christians and Muslims can worship together. In our world the panther still strikes. There is suffering and death.

In his letter to the Hebrews 2:5–12, Paul tells us we are meant for a better place. We need to fix our eyes on Jesus who leads the way and promises that we will share in his victory. Paul refers to Psalm 8 which always strikes a chord with me: "What are human beings that you [God] are mindful of them?" God is always mindful of us, and we need to be mindful of God.

The directions we need to follow to get to our true home are not that treacherous and difficult. But we should reflect on God's Word every day. Revelation can heal our souls and free our minds and hearts from the fears of this world. Paul says that Jesus "is not ashamed to call them brothers and sisters." He says that he will proclaim the father's name to us. All we need to do is listen to his word.

CHARTING A PATH

Sister Francis, a nun who taught me for three grades in high school, used to write a verse on the chalkboard on the first day of classes in the New Year:

> The New Year lies before you,
> like fresh-fallen snow;
> Be careful how you tread it,
> 'cause every step will show.

I still remember my debut as a farmer working the land. I was plowing a forty-acre field with a big tractor. I had studied natural science in school and learned about erosion prevention, so I tried to work around the big hill instead of driving in an overall rectangular pattern straight up and down the field. Well, it didn't work! Soon I was crisscrossing land I had already worked, and I was starting to be embarrassed by it all. Suppose someone saw me out here in broad daylight. It was turning into a "harrowing" experience.

Life is like that forty-acre field. There are choices and trade-offs. The inexperience of youth can account for much of our moral confusion. Theory never matches the demands of actual living. The angst of youth is real. Suppose someone could see our confusions and our sins? It is only with time and experience that we learn to control our impatience and confusion. With age comes serenity. Today I could work that forty-acre field with a good degree of skill. I can see the rectangular patterns, or if I choose, a diagonal pattern over the entire field. I can set my sights on a distant goal and drive a straight line to bisect the field.

With the passion and impatience of youth under control, our lives can experience a calm and peace. Our pattern of moral action becomes less erratic, closer to the way of perfection. We can start to work out the corners of our lives. We align ourselves more exactly with the Master's plan.

Fortunately we have a compassionate Master who gives us time, opportunity and inspiration as we work toward the harvest of our lives. What we sow in confusion we can reap in wisdom!

In Saskatchewan we tell a story about a traveler who asked a local farmer directions. The farmer began by saying, "Well, I wouldn't start out from here."

We are all lost sometimes; we're just not ready to admit it. The Good News is that we are never really lost. We are never really alone. We can start from anywhere, no matter how far we may have strayed from the right path. With just a little faith we could move mountains. And with a little love we can help each other find the way. We are always in God's hands. No night is too dark; no path is too difficult.

We all have our sins, but most of the time they are not made public. It takes real courage to admit, "I need help" or "I am an alcoholic." I have a plaque on my wall that shows a drunk man crawling along the ground and a saying in German that is translated: "No one sees my thirst, but everyone sees when I am drunk." As Christians, we know that God sees our thirst and is waiting to refresh us with living waters. It does not matter how many years we have been treading the wrong path, the right path is always just one step away.

After my mother washed our woolen socks in summer, we often had to spend time removing blue burrs that were embedded in the woolen fibers. The only way to remove them was to pick them out one by one with our fingernails. In the same way, our sinful habits tend to cling to us even when we have repented and been forgiven. Certain tendencies seem to cling.

The simple step that will put us back on the right path and deal with those latent tendencies toward sin is believing in God's love. If we could once believe and know the love God has for us, our attraction to sin would be less significant. Even our human failings would be less significant. It is only a change of heart that we need.

NOTES

i Eileen Danylczuk 1993—from *The Lamp*. Issue #26, March 2002.

Chapter Three

Meditation

For all time humans have been fascinated by the mysteries surrounding the eternal powers. From ancient druids to modern priests, we have generally relied on someone to interpret the mysteries that exist between God and us—to mediate our experience of the Divine. When death occurs, or when ultimate mysteries baffle us, we ask a minister to intervene and interpret reality for us.

But Christ came to change our relationship with the Almighty. God wants a personal relationship with you and me. We do not need to wait for intermediaries, but as a child to a parent, we should be open to interact with our God on a daily basis. God is always present. Are we?

God is ever near, ready to touch us in our daily lives. Saint Anselm (1033–1100) leaves us this instruction:

> Escape from your everyday business for a short while
> …Make a little time for God and rest a little while in
> him. Enter into your mind's inner chamber. Shut out
> everything but God…Speak now to God and say with
> your whole heart: "I seek your face; your face, Lord,
> I desire." [i]

In the quiet of our hearts God can shower us with joy for our sadness, peace for our anxiety. In this quiet meeting with God we will find strength against temptation. We can build on the rock of our salvation. Often our biggest temptation is simply to not trust in God and to avoid a meeting altogether. What is it that gives the deepest meaning to our lives?

Recently on a Saturday my wife was suffering the effects of the flu. I had my Saturday goals which included a number of things I wanted to do—work on my web page, write, pay some bills and other earth-shaking things. But I spent the day doing the things my wife would have done had she been feeling well—shopping and cleaning and family things. During the course of the day I felt energetic. I could feel energy pulsing through me. I even went jogging as well. And I came to the realization that Eric Little expressed so well in the movie *Chariots of Fire* when he talks about how he serves God using his ability to run: "When I run, I can feel his power in me." When we work for others, we can feel the energy of God in us. Whether it is looking after our family's needs or helping our neighbor, we truly can be the hands of Jesus. We truly can be a chariot of God, a vehicle that does God's work.

Imagine being a parent with a child who never talks to you. That is how God our Father feels when we don't talk to him. God has been revealing himself to humanity for over three thousand years—from walks in the cool of the evening in the Garden of Eden, through Abraham, Isaac and Jacob, Moses and the prophets. The Hebrew Scriptures are filled with hints about who God is and what God wants from and for us. The Incarnation, of course, is the most complete revelation of God to mankind. Jesus came to reveal many details of the Father's love to us, to model in his own flesh and blood the fullness of human life, and to offer himself for our shortcomings so that we might have life to the full.

You and I do not have to struggle to relate to God. It is God who waits for us. If we take advantage of the quiet moments in our day, perhaps before we get out of bed in the morning, while we wait in line or in traffic, stirring the coffee, packing a lunch—moments that we might have filled with worry or frustration—and offer a whispered prayer or even a moment's thought to God, our relationship will prosper. And once we have sought and found God in the quiet of our hearts, we must bring God to the world that has not yet learned how to seek him.

Even as God has been revealed to us in Scripture and in the Christian lives others have modeled for us, so we must be witnesses in our own lives of the peace that God offers to those who desire it. Out of his great love for us, God is still trying to reveal himself to mankind in the humanity of Jesus. We are called to model the humanity of Jesus, to be his hands, and feet, and voice. It is our greatest mission.

FINDING GOD IN NATURE

"Unless you...become like children, you will never enter the kingdom of heaven" (Matthew 18:3). One of the ways we can recapture our innocence, the innocence we had as children, is to revel in the wonders of the natural world.

Do we trust God as the King of the universe? Do we see his power at work in nature? Do we recognize him as the author and maintainer of the physical world?

Gerard Manley Hopkins, a Jesuit priest, in his poem "God's Grandeur" wrote that, "The world is charged with the grandeur of God (1)." Nature has a freshness and is constantly being renewed by the eternal forces: "Because the Holy Ghost over the bent / World broods with warm breast and with ah! Bright wings (13–14)."

In another poem "Pied Beauty" Hopkins gives us reason for great joy and self-acceptance. In the poem he praises God for "dappled things," for the "brinded cow," for the "stippled" fish. Each minute and each gigantic image of creation reflects the variety of things God has created. When I taught this poem to English classes over the years I used point out to the class that every one of us is different. Some of us have pimples; some have dimples. Our shapes are all different. Each one of us as a part of creation reflects the "variousness" (Hopkins's word) of things being different. Each one of us is a perfection of creation. I am the perfect shape, the perfect height, the perfect color for me. If I were anything else, I wouldn't be me. So praise God for the gift of my life, of your life!

Further in the poem, Hopkins discusses how the Holy Spirit permeates creation and "Father's forth" with the tremendous energy of creation. The world is constantly renewed and refreshed. Nature always renews the world according to God's plan.

Romantic poet William Wordsworth also sensed the presence of the eternal in nature. In "Lines" he says:

> ...I have felt...
> A presence that disturbs me with the joy
> Of elevated thoughts; a sense sublime
> Of something far more deeply interfused,...
> A motion and a spirit, that impels
> All thinking things, all objects of all thought,
> And rolls through all things. (93–102)

Recently I was caught on the golf course in a sudden thunderstorm. Fearful of lightning, I practically tiptoed to hide under the temporary shelter. No, my life did not flash before my eyes and I could not detect any of the signs that tell you when you are about to be zapped by lightning, but I did revisit the sweetest memory of boyhood when I was caught in a similar thunderstorm out in the cow pasture on my father's farm. I recalled the club moss that kept the dry prairie sod from eroding in the frequent winds or the infrequent downpour. I recalled the sweet scent on my fingers of the sage we used to create a smoky smudge to give the cows, horses and the odd sheep relief from the mosquitoes.

That summer shower gave me a few minutes from an exceptionally busy week of more work than time. In its twenty minutes it brought refreshing memories that spanned some forty years. For ever so brief a moment I had forgotten the rush of time and schedules. Nature and its author had been revisited.

TRANSCENDENTAL AND RELIGIOUS MEDITATION

Have you ever been a passenger in a car or bus, lulled by the humming tires or the sound of the road but not asleep, suddenly becoming alert and realizing that a half-hour has passed and you don't remember being conscious of it? You have just experienced something very similar to transcendental meditation (TM).

What is TM and how do you do it? Transcendental Meditation means transcending thought, going beyond present worries or concerns. TM is a technique that clears the mind of thought and enables the subject to experience a deep rest in a short time—twenty minutes or less. The measurement of brainwave activity during TM suggests the subject is at deep rest, such as in an eight-hour sleep. A mantra may be used to induce relaxation. A mantra is a sound or thought which, when repeated, allows the subject to forget all else. Some subjects listen to a sound like their breathing, or a fan motor, while others concentrate on a mental image.

How do you meditate? It is very simple. Find a quiet place, free from distractions. Sit in a comfortable position, head unsupported. Good posture will help you focus your attention and reduce the risk of falling asleep. Close your eyes. Clear your mind. The ideal state is the absence of thought. A mantra may be used. Meditation in the morning and again after the day's work to prepare yourself for the evening is suggested. TM is best before a meal, not after; after exercise it is excellent.

You don't have time to do it? TM allows you to get away with less sleep, adding rest periods during the day when you need it most. A timer may be used if time is limited. Even skeptics concede that everyone would benefit from taking twenty minutes twice a day to relax.

The secret to successful meditation is tranquility of heart and soul. Poet Leonard Cohen talks about each morning trying to find a "state of grace," a place in his mind where there is calm. From there creativity is possible.

William Wordsworth talks about pastoral scenes such as the banks of the Wye River (from "Lines") and stores these in his mind for use "amid the din of towns and cities." Then, as he recalls the scenes they pass "into my purer mind, with tranquil restoration" (29–30). Later he describes what sounds like the physical state of deep relaxation during meditation:

> ...the motion of our human blood
> Almost suspended, we are laid asleep

In body, and become a living soul:
While with an eye made quiet by the power
Of harmony, and the deep power of joy,
We see into the life of things. (44–49)

Those who meditate have long talked about experiences such as "being in touch with the universe" and "a blissful consciousness." To the mystics this means inner peace and harmony with God. Transcendental Meditation (TM) can become a deeply religious experience. Once you are familiar with the process, the next step is simple. Get into a comfortable position, close your eyes, and put yourself into God's presence. This may be easier than you think. Consider for a moment that every breath of air is a gift from God. Most of us are blessed with the ability to breathe without pain—a greater gift. Breathe deeply and slowly, listening to God's energy and gift in you. Say "thank you" for each breath. You have just established a mantra. This may work for you.

Simply putting yourself into God's hands and relaxing is another approach. Whatever troubles and worries you have been carrying, simply give them into God's hands. You have carried them long enough without help. God will take them and you will experience peace. Relax.

The whole concept of religious meditation is only logical if you are at peace with God, however you perceive him or her. You must find the "state of grace" where your soul finds true peace. The process of daily interaction with the eternal force will become easier with practice. God is a fast learner! We may fumble awkwardly for awhile. Practice! Practice! Once we get the hang of it, it becomes easier, the process simpler.

ZEN REFLECTIONS
Where is God? Our perception of God is somewhere on a continuum between not being fully convinced of his existence, on the one hand, and taking him for granted, on the other hand. If you were walking down a forest path and you found four sticks arranged in a perfect square, what would you surmise? Obviously that someone had passed

by, someone with intelligence. When you look at the complexity of the human eye, or consider the billions of neurons in the brain, what do you surmise about its creator?

In a recent article in *Time* magazine, a comparison is made between the construction of a skyscraper and the development of a child in the womb:

> Imagine yourself as the world's tallest skyscraper, built in nine months and germinating from a single brick. As that brick divides, it gives rise to every other type of material needed to construct and operate the finished tower—a million tons of steel, concrete, mortar, insulation, tile, wood, solvents, carpet, cable, pipe and glass as well as all furniture, phone systems, heating and cooling units, plumbing, electrical wiring, artwork and computer networks, including software.... Given the number of steps in the process, it will perhaps forever seem miraculous that life ever comes into being without a major hitch.[ii]

Einstein said, "Look at the stars and learn [about the creator]." Simply gazing at the stars at night or walking through a forest or a park can unveil so much beauty that we think of God's goodness and love.

But God is close to us in the humdrum activities and struggles of daily life. Father François Fenelon, a medieval mystic in the Court of King Louis XIV, was keenly aware of the pressures of daily living when he taught, "You must not wait for disengaged hours, when you can close your door and see nobody.... Immediately turn your heart to God, simply, familiarly, and trustfully. Wherever God may lead you, there you will find him, in the most harassing business as in the most tranquil prayer."

As creature to creator, we need to turn frequently and say, "Thank you, God," or we need to say, "Help me God." We need not wait for the awe-inspiring moments that come so rarely as a holiday from work. But just in case we need a reminder, we have the daily sunrise, sunset, starlight and other gifts too numerous to mention.

This does not mean that we should imagine that all lives are composed of one inspirational event after another. There is a Hindu saying: "The lotus flower grows in the mud / The deeper the mud, the more beautiful the flower." A perennial that is always with us, always blooming, is the flower of despair and depression in our lives. Anxiety is a constant of the human condition. Jesus habitual greeting was, "Peace be with you" (John 20:20) or "Do not be afraid" (Matthew 28:10). Jesus raised Lazarus from the very death we universally fear as part of our human condition. The greater death to fear is the death of sin, which kills the Spirit in us. Jesus wants to free us from that death also. "Repent, and believe the good news" (Mark 1:15).

Jesus went into the most hopeless darkness that a human can face. He accepted death with all the physical pain and the human despair that caused him to cry out, "My God, my God, why have you forsaken me?" Because of Christ, it is easier for us to face death. We have the absolute physical evidence of the Resurrection and the Spirit in our world to inspire us and to give us joy. Further, the astounding fact of Christ's Resurrection is our hope. The Father raised him just as he will raise what is immortal inside us. Just as Martha said, "Yes, Lord, I believe that you are the Christ, the Son of God" (John 11:27), so we also proclaim the Risen Lord. This is what enables us to come out of the slime and mud of mortal existence and to blossom into a beautiful lotus flower.

According to Greek legend, the lotus fruit caused a dreamy and contented forgetfulness to those who ate it. In truth, our faith blossoming in the Resurrected Lord will help us leave fear and despair behind. We will be able to continue our lives with hope and joy. The Good News that we share, you and I, is that the Risen Christ will restore what was dead in us and raise us up to new life. I know it is his wish. We no longer need to fear. We only need to accept.

Like the story of the Zen master who said to the hot dog vendor, "Make me one with everything," the full implication of our connection to everything gives us both a challenge and hope. How we are one with each other has the effect of ripples in a pond. Thomas Merton leads us in one direction when he says:

There is not one of us, individually, racially, socially who is fully complete in the sense of having in one-self all the excellence of humanity. And this excel-lence, this totality, is built up out of the contributions of the particular parts of it that we all can share with one another. I am therefore not completely human until I have found myself in my African and Asian and Indonesian brothers and sisters because they have the part of humanity which I lack.[iii]

When Saint Stephen was martyred, one of the young men present was Saint Paul who was persecuting Christians at the time: "and the wit-nesses laid their coats at the feet of a young man named Saul" (Acts 7). Here we see the positive effects of the event of Jesus' incarnation which dropped like a pebble into a pond. The ripples set into motion by Christ filled Stephen with "grace and power" so he worked "won-ders and signs among the people." Stephen forgave his killers in his dying breath.

Saint Paul heard Stephen's final witness: "I see the heavens opened and the Son of man standing at the right hand of God." The *spoken* word, the witness given, has the effect of a pebble on a pond. Saul goes on to conversion and a Spirit-filled ministry.

To be one with everything puts us in touch with the influences of others, like Stephen and Paul and Christ. It also challenges us to be discerning in the ripples we send out to others.

Too often we underestimate our importance; we think we are worthless and insignificant. But look around. Can you see anyone else who is insignificant? Look at any parent, brother, sister, friend, sen-ior. Everyone is vital and plays a key role in the fabric of society. It seems to us that we are the only insignificant failures around. The good news is that when we feel like this we are so totally wrong. The proof, logically, lies in the many eyes of all those around us who see our significance. We are vital in the fabric of society.

It gets better! When God looks at us, he sees someone so significant that he would let his own son die for us. That is a mystery of pure love. To die for someone we love would be difficult, but to die for a stranger or an enemy? Obviously we are neither of these to God. If we have even a partial understanding of God's love for us and his plan in Jesus, then we could feel like the disciples when Jesus left them to ascend to heaven: "While he was blessing them, he withdrew from them and was carried up into heaven. And they worshiped him, and returned to Jerusalem with great joy; and they were continually in the temple blessing God" (Luke 24:51–53).

The followers of Jesus feel joy. Even though he is leaving them, they understand their mission. They go back to their work with great joy. You and I need to live that Ascension joy today: "While he is blessing us, he withdraws from us to ascend into heaven. And we worship him, and we go about our daily lives with great joy; and we are continually going to church praising God."

This world has been redeemed. The victory is already won, though we may not see it yet. The Holy Spirit moves in us and in the world, and creation is becoming the "Kingdom of Our Lord, and of His Christ," as Handel expresses it in the Hallelujah chorus. Mankind gives the earth a particular purpose, direction and a conscious freedom. Because of us the world has a history and is a history. Every human has dignity and individual purpose in the mind of God, the creator. We are not just a large, impersonal, collective reality, but each of us has a particular purpose, existence and redemption. Just as we believe in the significance and importance of each individual in a democratic society, so we must know the uniqueness and preciousness of our individual selves in the mind of God. The more we think about it, the more exciting God and eternity become.

NOTES

[i] Saint Anselm, "Desire for the Vision of God."

[ii] J. Madeleine Nash, "Inside the Womb," *Time*, November 11, 2002.

[iii] Thomas Merton, cited in *Prairie Messenger*, January 10, 2001.

CHAPTER FOUR

The Good News

To many of us "Good News" would be winning the lottery or having Publisher's Clearinghouse stop at our front door. I heard a story about a righteous man in financial distress who prayed to win the lottery. Week after week, his prayers grew ever more urgent and his frustration ever more evident. Finally, after years of patience, he yells at the heavens, "I've done everything you've ever asked of me, every day of my life! Could you at least answer my prayer one time and *let me win the lottery*?" And a voice came from the sky: "Could you at least buy a ticket?" If we want to participate tangibly in the Good News, we've got to buy a ticket. We have to go to church regularly, make time for daily prayer and reflection on Scripture. We have to transform our lives completely.

The "big one" is already won. Christ died on the cross to give us that eternal reward. Christ died for sinners, not for the just. The Good News should bring tremendous joy to our world. But Christians often fail to embrace all that jubilation.

Researchers in one study reported that children laugh up to four hundred times a day, while adults laugh a mere fifteen times a day. We have lost 385 laughs a day!

Playboy magazine once published a picture of a laughing Christ. It depicted Jesus with his head thrown back in joyful laughter. A number of irate letters were received accusing the magazine of being irreverent and of trivializing Christ. What a sad commentary on how Christianity through the ages has passed on the "Gospel" or "Good News." The greatest cause of sorrow and sadness in the world has been overcome. Christ has conquered death and sin. Hope springs eternally for us. We cannot be sad if we keep sight of the eternal truths.

An old Jewish proverb says: "Anyone who sees a legitimate pleasure and does not enjoy it is an ingrate against God who made it possible." Yes, we should enjoy the pleasures and gifts of the earth the creator has made for us. In the Kingdom we will all be like little children again. We will laugh, and all sorrow will be banished. The final image of Christ we will see is Christ at the eternal banquet feast, with his head thrown back in joyful laughter, celebrating with us. With our limited imaginations it may already be possible for us to see that Christ is the same yesterday, today and for all eternity. The heavenly banquet feast is already in progress. We indeed have a cause to celebrate!

Joy comes in measure with faith. God is still with us in the same way he was during the life of Christ. But wouldn't faith be so much easier if we could witness some manifestation from the world beyond our world? Just a little miracle now and then and we would believe beyond a doubt. There are signs and wonders in abundance all around us. All we need to do is be attuned to them.

I want to share several examples of miracles, beginning with a little story about angels from a writer and editor of a small paper in Clinton, Indiana. Before he enters the newsroom rush each morning, he pauses outside on the sidewalk to take a breath of fresh air and offer a little prayer of thanks. In his words: "One day last year I looked up, and hovering over me, spanning the blue sky, was an angel formed from clouds! Journalists deal with facts, and I carefully noted what I was seeing—well-defined wings covered with snowy-white feathers, and a long gown, light and flowing. I think that the beautiful sky-wide angel was God's gift to me for appreciating each day he's created (from *Angels On Earth*, Sept./Oct. 1998)."

There are signs from the world beyond—miraculous healing, interventions from angels, and often occurrences in our lives that are slightly beyond coincidence. But we forget so readily. In Jesus' parable about Lazarus and the rich man, the rich man cries out from Hades: "Father [Abraham], I beg you to send Lazarus to my father's house—for I have five brothers—that he may warn them, so that they do not come to this place of torment." Abraham replies, "If they do not listen to Moses and the prophets, neither will they be convinced even if someone rises from the dead." How about you and me? Do we listen to someone who actually rose from the dead?

I have heard from a very reliable witness about a faith-healing that involved the sudden death of a baby. The mother refused to accept this as God's will. She prayed and carried on long past the point of reason and logic. Bystanders were expressing shock and becoming scandalized at her behavior. She continued pleading with the Lord. The child suddenly came back to life. Yet this is a small miracle compared to one who actually came back to life on his own accord.

A saintly man once told me of a miraculous healing of a Ukrainian dancer who was to perform in Winnipeg. He had a broken ankle. After being prayed over, his leg was healed. Ask ten people around you if any of them have been witnesses to some small miracle in their lives or in the lives of a loved one. We are surrounded with the little miracles of life. All that is needed is some introspection, some time to reflect on the deeper meanings. Suddenly faith is not such a big leap.

Have you seen "signs and wonders," some little miracles that have reminded you about the ultimate realities of God and his tremendous love for us? I have. In John 4:48 Jesus says to the stubborn people of his hometown of Galilee: "So you will not believe unless you see signs and wonders." He does go on to show them a sign and to cure the court official's son. The reality is that miracles are still going on around us. There are incredible healings and events that defy mere coincidence.

Several times I have missed a minor or major accident in life and simply turned and said, "Thank you, Dad." I associate my father with anything that relates to cars, especially older cars that are difficult to keep in repair. Dad had a great deal of experience with such cars during his life. Several times on our winter holiday trips through

Saskatoon our old car broke down in the city, a couple of times precisely at the service station across from McDonald's on 22nd Street. It was almost a family tradition. The family would eat while I got the mechanic to get us roadworthy again. Twice, when repairs were major, we enjoyed the hospitality of my sister in Saskatoon. I thank Providence and Dad for not getting stranded on the highway.

Once on a trip to Regina for a Lay Ministries training weekend, I was heading towards Balgonie as dusk was falling. I had just finished praying a rosary and was thinking of passing a slow-moving truck ahead of me. I decided for the moment not to rush. Just then a car passed from the front with no lights on. There was no way I would have seen that car if I had passed. "Thank you, Dad."

On a Christmas holiday at Eston, Saskatchewan, some years back, our baby had severe congestion and was struggling to breathe. We had elevated one side of the crib to facilitate breathing. Late that night I asked my mother for help. It was Grandma's turn to help, I thought, and she was in heaven; what could it hurt? The baby slept through the next feeding and was breathing so quietly, I got out of bed in alarm to check for breathing. "Thank you, Mom."

One of the most touching signs I experienced occurred after the death of a young man in Canora. The June following his accidental death his family was attending Sunday Mass on the weekend of the graduation of one of the children. I was assisting the presider as a minister of the Eucharist, distributing Holy Communion. I watched the family approach to receive the Eucharist. As I glanced up at the mother, I noticed an image of her late husband above her and to her left. I can still see the smile on his face. He was still with his family. A long time passed before I shared this with anyone.

Signs are important reminders to us of deeper spiritual realities. There are many examples in the Bible: the rainbow in Genesis, the tongues of fire in Corinthians, or the pillar of fire in Exodus. We need to attune ourselves to recognize the little signs and miracles in our everyday lives. God should be an exciting reality for us, not some comforting fable to remember in times of fear or sadness.

THOUGHTS OF LOVE

Love can be subject to the greatest misunderstanding, but the good news is that love persists. Sometimes when lovers quarrel, it is only because they love each other that one or perhaps both feel betrayed. If there were no love, they would react with indifference rather than anger. We are most wounded when we feel that one we love has betrayed us. When we get past the hurt of pride and once again recognize and accept an unconditional love, the relationship is secure.

Recently I have been reflecting on one important question: Is God pleased with me? Only on the best days can I admit that maybe he is. The fault in perception is mine. The mistrust of pride is mine. I don't trust enough in God's love to turn myself over. I come back to self-judgment: Am I pleased with me?

The Good News is that God loves us unconditionally (it's even hard to believe this as I say it). Let me offer some proof. My parents loved me unconditionally. Sometimes I disappointed them; sometimes they had to instruct me or punish me. But I always knew my place in our home was guaranteed and reserved for me. At the end of the day I had a banquet (supper) and a place to rest. Loving arms were there to hug me and tuck me in. Were my parents pleased with me? Of course they were. And because of them, I could be pleased with myself.

Is God not a better parent than our parents are? Parents are not perfect—I am a parent and I know. Yet, imperfect as we are, we do not disown our children for their lack of perfection, but we continue to pray for them and gently lead them toward a higher love. In Isaiah 49:1 we read:

> The LORD called me before I was born
> while I was in my mother's womb he named me.

The entire passage reaffirms the message: "I have inscribed you on the palms of my hands" (49:16). Even if our human parents can abandon us, God will not:

> Can a woman forget her nursing child,
> or show no compassion for the child of her womb?

Even these may forget,
  yet I will not forget you. (49:15)

The passage ends with this assurance: "Then all flesh shall know that I am the LORD your Savior" (49:26).

We are precious in the eyes of God! We can live our lives with the assurance that at the end of our day on earth there is a place for us. God has prepared a banquet for us, and we have a place to rest. Loving arms will be there to hug us and to tuck us in. "Precious in the sight of the LORD / is the death of his faithful ones" (Psalm 116:15).

The joy of human love is aptly illustrated in the movie *City of Angels* when an angel (Nicholas Cage) falls in love with a human (Meg Ryan) and decides to become mortal. Shortly after this the character played by Ryan dies. A companion asks Cage if he had known how it was going to end, would he have done it, now that he faces a lonely human existence and eventual death. Cage replies: "One breath of her hair, one kiss of her mouth, one touch of her hand is better than an eternity without it."

How much we take our loved ones for granted! How much we fail to treasure the dawn, the sunset, the touch of a rose, the experience of all that appeals to our human senses. To be able to breathe without pain, to feel well and complete—we take so much for granted. In Thornton Wilder's play *Our Town,* Emily, who has come back from the grave, asks the question: "Do any human beings ever realize life while they live it? Every, every minute?" The Stage Manager replies, "No. The saints and poets, maybe—they do some."

There is a value above all price for the smallest events in our daily lives. The human state is next to that of God. Our free will places us above the angels. Our redemption by Christ restores what we have lost through sin, original and unoriginal. As humans we often make a mess of our personal lives. We only need to repent, to turn back toward the love of God, and believe the Good News, and we will truly rejoice in a rich, meaningful and human existence!

There is a story about a man with a curious affliction. He complains to his friend, "I'm always seeing Elvis Presley. I see him in a crowd; I see him in the window of a passing bus, and I see him in the oddest places." "Have you seen a psychiatrist?" his friend asks. "No, just Elvis!" Elvis still has a great following. Rumors of sightings are frequent. People visit his gravesite like a shrine. Christians should have a different vision, and that is seeing Christ. We should see him frequently. Not only that, but we should be telling others about him. Even more important than seeing Christ around us is *being* Christ to others. Christ came to serve. In your home, he is the first to volunteer to start that huge stack of dishes. He takes out the garbage. He cleans up the environment. He visits the shut-ins. Just keep your eyes open; you'll see him. Keep your heart open and you'll *be* him.

GO TELL EVERYONE

What do you do when you find a great bargain at the grocery store? Do you tell someone about it? What if you've just seen a great movie, perhaps the greatest you've ever seen? Do you tell anyone about it? Someone has invented a new automotive fuel—easily accessible, virtually inexhaustible and absolutely free! Would you tell your friends about it?

The examples are trivial, even insignificant, compared to our eternal realities. When you and I discover an eternal truth; when we discern a better way or path to the Father, do we tell anyone about it? We are given the gift of faith and hope. Do we tell anyone about it? The gift of love is a different matter. Love speaks volumes. If we love, it covers over many a sin (1 Peter 4:8). It is hard to keep love a secret. Our genuine care for others, our knowledge of their worth as redeemed members of the family of Christ, makes it difficult to be silent about the Good News. Our actions speak volumes. The message of Christ expressed through the action of Christian love is hard to refuse.

Sometimes we hesitate; we fail to show the action that a loving Christian should. Sometimes we fail to remember how we are the beloved of Christ, how we can help others though we are sinners. Let me give an example. In Morley Callaghan's novel *Such Is My Beloved* we are left with two ideas about the significance of the title. The "beloved" could refer to Christ at the Transfiguration when the Father's voice says: "This is my Son, the Beloved; with him I am well pleased" (Matthew 17:5). Father Dowling in the story is like Christ in that he seeks to help two prostitutes at the risk of scandal and even persecution from his own church. The other interpretation of "the beloved" in the story could simply be that the sinners, like the two prostitutes in the story, are the beloved of Christ. I prefer the latter interpretation, but both are correct. Our God is one who not only seeks the sinner, but he also wants to communicate the need for us to be like Christ. To be the beloved of God is to be like Christ!

We are, of course, somewhat less than Christ. Our mortal nature has us struggling with imperfections. We fail as much as we succeed. But we go on, as wounded healers, with God's grace. To serve God whom we cannot see, we simply must serve our neighbor whom we can see. We need to stand for something in this world. The singer is as essential as the song or the message. There are many who do not buy or accept the gospel as the Good News of Christ. Could it be that there is something about the singer (us) that interferes with the song?

Love is a gift from our Creator. The opportunities to make this a better world are all around. We aren't always faced with situations that call for the heroics of the moment, like those who find themselves the subject of TV dramas. No, you and I are tested more seriously. We need constant courage to face everyday life and to face all the struggles and challenges that test us when we are worn out and frayed.

At the end of this day we might ask ourselves: "What really changed the world today? Was it the actions of the United Nations? Was it what happened in Washington or New York, London or Beijing? Was it Middle East diplomacy?" No! It was in fact the good men and women and children of God and all the little acts of kindness and love that they performed. That's what really helped to make a difference in the world today!

When we imagine that our roles are insignificant, that we have little to contribute as heralds of the Good News, we must remember the depth of each human deed. Remember a time when someone—perhaps a relative or friend, perhaps even a total stranger—offered you a word or gesture that changed your life. We have all experienced these graced moments.

It is our calling to be constantly vigilant, looking for opportunities to do the work of Christ, and to be open to the inspiration of the Holy Spirit, so that we might not only be receivers, but proclaimers, of the Good News.

CHAPTER FIVE

Favorite Inspirations

THE LORD IS MY SHEPHERD

Occasionally in my column *Pause for Reflection* I have used titles that come with a great deal of emotional attachment, titles such as "When the Saints Go Marching in," "Faith of our Fathers," "The Lord is My Shepherd" and "Tradition!" Each of these has a song attached, and he who sings, prays twice. In this chapter I will share some of these favorite inspirations.

When the Saints Go Marching In has always reminded me of one of the most moving passages in Scripture that gives us great hope, the vision of John in Revelation 7:9–14: "After this I looked, and there was a great multitude that no one could count, from every nation, from all tribes and peoples and languages, standing before the throne and before the Lamb.... Then one of the elders addressed me, saying, "Who are these, robed in white, and where have they come from?" It is with great joy that I picture many whom I have known in this world standing in that assembly. There are my parents, my father-in-law, my grandparents, two sisters, a brother-in-law, some friends from Canora who have passed on, and the list goes on. You can picture some who are there. These are the saints. Not the big saints like Peter and Paul, but ordinary people like you and me. People who believed and persisted in their good works, and were redeemed by the love of Christ.

I know I am a sinner. Some days I do foolish things. If you are close enough to me, you have seen my warts. I'm not perfect, yet. Some days I know the Lord must shake his head a little, perhaps smile and say, "What's he up to today?" Sometimes we are foolish. But the Lord has led us so far along life's path that he doesn't want to lose us now. Even when we lose our direction, he persists. Oh, did I mention? God talks to himself sometimes. It's not meant to be that way, but sometimes we just aren't listening.

How many times do we read in the Bible or hear a preacher say, "Believe and repent!" That seems redundant to me. If we believe, we will repent. The love of God for us leaves no alternative. As we grow closer to the Lord, we will naturally turn away from sin. We cannot go in two directions at once, even if we have two faces. If this chapter appears glib or flippant in places, I make no apologies. As we experience the love of God and grow closer to God, it will make us giddy. "Lord, I want to be in that number! When the saints go marching in."

Faith of Our Fathers is a title that rivets our focus on what is most precious and has been carried in trust by our parents, their parents and their grandparents, and so on, in my case, back to Russia and further back to Germany. Sometimes we fail to realize that the choices we make about our faith lives affect not only us, but many around us and generations to come. My great grandparents came from Saratov, Russia, where they and their ancestors lived for over one hundred years. Before that they had come from Germany at the invitation of Catherine the Great to teach the Russian farmers western (European) farming methods.

I can trace the roots of my faith journey from Germany to Russia, from Russia to Cactus Lake (Saskatchewan), from Cactus Lake to Canora. Generation after generation has passed on much culture, language, values, faith, a way of life. The challenge is for this generation to succeed in the same faith transaction. Are we making the kind of choices that will beget another generation of faith?

The church today—institutional religion in general—seems to be having a real struggle. Sure, we all still find the church handy for weddings, baptisms and funerals. But too often it does not serve much purpose in between. The present generation is treading on thin ice when it comes to faith. Many of us still understand the rituals and ceremonies. Will the next generation have the same rich legacy?

Are our church ministers up to the challenge of occasional cate-
chesis? Instructions once or twice a year? Is this generation so gifted
that we can pick up and learn the faith of our fathers from such limited exposure? What about our grandchildren? Who is supporting the
church they will need? This applies to both the financial matters and
ecclesiastical structures. The answers to these questions are the same
as the answer Moses gave the Israelites on Mount Horeb: "Choose
life, then, so that you and your descendants may live, in the love of
Yahweh your God."

Tradition! In the movie *Fiddler on the Roof* the question is raised
as to why young people should follow the beliefs and values of their
elders. The answer is "Tradition!" This force binds us so powerfully
that we will fight to uphold tradition and model our lives after it. My
hometown Canora is a community rich in tradition. The older generation has faithfully tried to pass on language, values, customs, music,
songs and stories. The annual Veselka Dance Concert is an illustration of what is great in tradition. Young lads and maidens are enact-
ing the stories of life. Some are so young they fail to grasp the deeper
nuances, but others shed real tears with the realization of the richness
of the culture they are expressing.

I have the utmost respect for the cultural heritage of others. Sadly,
many of my cultural traditions have been lost in my generation. My
German ancestors lived in Russia for more than a hundred years and
safeguarded their language, customs and religion while living there.
It was because of their privileged position that they eventually were
persecuted and their lands taken by the Russian people. To escape
this persecution they immigrated to Canada. To make sure that this
persecution would not be repeated in Canada, my ancestors decided
to learn and adopt the language and culture of the new country. Much
of the richness of these Russian-German people was lost in a single
generation. The saddest aspect of this loss was that many of the values disappeared as well. Tradition and customs of a people deserve
the deepest respect. They are tied to the profoundest values of a people. The language articulates the songs and stories that are the soul of
a people. Tradition!

One of the favorite all-time Bible passages and one which brings us the greatest consolation is Psalm 23, "The Lord Is My Shepherd." At the time of death we can hope to hear the voice of the shepherd calling us. It is one of life's great experiences to recognize the voice of a loved one. At a time of loneliness, the voice of a lover consoles, transforms us. How sweet to recognize that voice.

As a child I remember on occasion hearing my father's voice after he had been away on what seemed a long absence. Today I realize it was just a week of Convention of the Saskatchewan Association of Rural Municipalities, but as a child missing my father and worrying about his return through a March blizzard, it was a great consolation to hear his voice. Specifically, on one occasion, I first knew of his return when I heard his cough from the back of the church. What a consoling sound that cough was, to know he had returned safely and my world was secure again.

In John 10 Jesus says, "I am the good shepherd. I know mine and mine know me...they listen to my voice." Sheep will listen to a shepherd's voice when he calls them away from the edge of a precipice, away from danger. They will follow his voice when it is too dark to see. To many of us the most consoling words in the Bible are Psalm 23:

> The LORD is my shepherd, I shall not want.
>   He makes me lie down in green pastures;
> he leads me beside still waters;
>   he restores my soul.
> He leads me in right paths for his name's sake.
>
> Even though I walk through the darkest valley,
>   I fear no evil.

At the time of death of a loved one, we hear these consoling words. Hopefully at the time of our own death, we will hear the voice of the shepherd when we are in the valley of darkness, right after we say, "Into your hands I commend my spirit." But until that day comes, we have to accomplish one small task. We must learn to recognize the voice of the shepherd. Recognizing the master's voice begins early in life. It is experienced as a child when we hear the consoling voice of a parent when we are afraid of the dark. It is heard during youth when the quiet inner voice says, "That is wrong. This is the right path." It is heard as a young adult when someone says, "I love you," and forges a bond of trust and love that can withstand loneliness, separation and times of trial. A good spouse is a gift from God and a helpmate on the journey to the Father.

Daily prayer and moments of silence with the Lord can lead us to recognize the inner prompting and calling of God our Father. He sent his Son to instruct us and he sent his Spirit to guide us through this valley of darkness. We need to grow closer to our Lord through the trials of this life so we will hear and recognize his voice. What a great consolation to know that at the moment of greatest need, during the final trials of life, the same voice that led us to green pastures and has given us rest in the special moments of grace in this world, will also hail us from the darkness and lead us to the banquet table prepared for us. It will be a wilderness no longer. All suffering will be gone. Every tear will be wiped away.

WALKING ON WATER

There is a story about a Catholic priest, a Protestant minister, and an atheist who were out in a boat on the lake one morning talking about walking on water. Both of the men of the cloth were confident that their faith was strong and they would give it a try. The atheist believed that the task could be accomplished by using "mind over matter." The Protestant minister went first and made it all the way across the water to the shore. Next the scoffing atheist hopped out of the boat and virtually skipped across the water. At last the priest stepped out nervously, and sank like a stone. As his companions watched him struggling, the atheist turned to the minister and asked, "Do you think we should tell him where the rocks are?"

You and I need to walk on water. We do that metaphorically when we call out to Jesus as we are sinking in the trials of life. Saint Peter needed Jesus to pull him up when he tried walking on water (Matthew 14:31). We may fall as we learn to walk in faith, but Jesus is there to help us up and tell us where the rocks are. Saint Peter is an interesting study. In his failings he reminds me of myself in some ways. "Even though I must die with you, I will not deny you" (Matthew 26:35), he says. Then later, when things get really tough and he needs to stand up for what is right: "I do not know the man," he says. Yet with God's help and the infusion of the Holy Spirit, Peter does go bravely as a witness to Christ and is eventually crucified.

There are Gethsemanes in our lives, situations of temptation and trial: a loved one commits suicide; a son or daughter is alienated and runs away from home; a habit of drugs or sin takes over our free will. At these times we need to cry out to the Lord like Peter did and Jesus will give us the strength we need. It will not necessarily be easy. There are no magic tricks, no rocks to walk on. We will need real faith. That is what saved Peter in the end. It is when things are going well for us that we have a false sense of security and we feel that we really do not need the Lord. Like Peter, we need to learn from our sins.

We need to strive for a simple trust in God and to not put our security in our property and wealth. We often see news stories about earthquakes or floods in Third World countries, and we see life there at a simpler level. The poor often have all their belongings packed on their backs as they move to start a new life. We would need several moving vans to move all of our accumulated baggage. In Matthew 17:27 we see Jesus solving a financial problem for Peter. Peter was asking Jesus about the temple tax. Jesus told him to cast his net into the sea, take the first fish that came up, and in its mouth Peter would find a coin to pay the tax collectors.

Compare the story in Matthew with a modern inner-city church that accumulated more than two million dollars in a building fund for that day sometime in the future when they might need to build a new church. The church was in good repair; income was decidedly more than expenses, and yet the parish was hoarding a fortune, some of which rightfully should have gone to the desperately needy right in their own city. We need to ask God for our needs more frequently. At a simple, humble level we need to trust in God. The same Jesus who solved Peter's problem with a coin in a fish's mouth can provide for our needs, not all of which are related to money. The poor, of necessity, trust in God. The more affluent tend to trust in themselves. Is it surprising that the message of Christ is more welcome among developing nations who look forward to the promise of the gospel: "Happy are the poor in spirit, theirs is the kingdom of heaven"?

Our struggle to meet the challenges of daily living is one that can be reduced to very simple terms. Life is a journey. Several years ago, I paused to reflect on a young mother pushing a baby carriage before her. As she walked down the sidewalk she was also vigilantly conscious of an older child also in her care, walking behind her. She was on one aspect of her life's journey and doing a great job. She had purpose and meaning, but did she know it? You and I are on a similar journey. Our day-to-day work makes us responsible for certain aspects of this world. But there is one significant area of our trip we should not neglect, and that is the philosophic base that makes life worth living.

"Life sucks" is something we hear from some of our youth today. If we listen longer we may hear the rejoinder remark, "And then you die." Poet William Wordsworth speaks of age "that brings the philosophic mind." We need that. Life has to have meaning, be grounded in a value system, so we don't end up saying: "Is that all there is?"

One of the problems some of us experience is that we are too busy to think. Especially when we are young, rather than internalizing life's experiences and establishing a personal value system, we fill our time with CDs, the Internet, mp3 players, school, work. There is no time for introspection!

Usually, as we grow older, we sense that there is a deeper meaning to life. We want a spiritual dimension to give us meaning. In the play *Our Town* Thornton Wilder says that deep down everyone knows there is something eternal about us. The wisest men have been telling us this for the last three thousand years. Yet we keep forgetting about it. The good news is that, for most of us, life is long. We have years to grow out of our childhoods, to be prepared to assume an adult role. Then we have years of living as an adult, gradually adding a spiritual depth to our lives. In the Talmud we get the following words of wisdom: "Old age is winter to the foolish, / Harvest to the wise." If we seek wisdom throughout our lives, surely we will rejoice in the harvest of age.

CHAPTER SIX

Church

Irish comedian Hal Roach observes about the Christian values governing physical love of a dating couple: "Certain actions are forbidden until they are compulsory!"

In an ideal marriage there would be no need to think of physical sharing as "compulsory." The question would never come up. A wife and husband are there for each other and build all aspects of their relationship. They use God's gift of sexual love to enhance their closeness and oneness. There is excitement even when one is merely in the presence of the other.

Similarly in a good Christian life, the "obligation" of Sunday worship should never come up. And the opportunities of enhancing our love relationship with God are even more generous. We are free to pursue an intimate relationship with God in our daily lives. If we love God and get to know God, we naturally want to add to our relationship by attendance at Sunday or even daily services. We look for sacramental nourishment as we seek ways to expand our union with God.

What makes a good church? Often we hear more about what is wrong with the church. But we must realize that all who profess to be Christian are the church! We cannot point a finger at problems in the church and say, "You know what is wrong with the church? If only *they* would do such and such..."

The fact is that Christ established the church to carry out his work on earth. He appointed disciples to spread the word, and he sent his spirit to guide future Pentecosts and maintain the life of his body on earth. Peter is the rock or cornerstone. Saint Paul talks about us as being "members" of Christ's body on earth (1 Corinthians 12). The church is not just a building, is not just clergy. All baptized Christians are the church.

There is also a broader challenge involved in membership in the Christian church. Christ is not just a local experience. The church is universal and has stood through the ages—from Edinburgh to Rome, from Constantinople to Jerusalem. At a time when we can count more than four thousand non-Christian centers (Internet statistic) in the United States alone, it is important that we take more seriously our role as Christ's body on earth. And it is high time we worked together as a united body doing the work of Christ on earth. After all, we are church.

Jesus established the church as a way of his continued presence on earth, his loving arms still present for us. Many today have drifted away from that presence and are lost to the opportunities it presents. Let me illustrate with the story of a man who climbed a tree during a flood. He clung for safety as the water rose. A boat came by offering help. He said, "No. I'm going to trust that God will save me." A helicopter came by, but again the man refused to be rescued. Finally the rising waters drowned him. When he met up with God he asked, "How come you didn't help me?" God replied, "Well, I sent a boat and a helicopter!"

The man in this story was obviously out of touch with God. To bear fruit on the vine of Christ we need to seek constant nourishment. This generation may be remembered for its forgetting about going to church, to the banquet of Christ that can nourish us on a weekly or daily basis. You and I are often out of touch with the Lord, but God keeps on intervening in our lives. One way that God does this is by "pruning" actions, much like that of a gardener in spring. In John 15 Jesus says: "I am the true vine, and my Father is the vinegrower. He removes every branch in me that bears no fruit. Every branch that bears fruit he prunes to make it bear more fruit." This is one of the great analogies in the Bible. It is as powerful as the comparison of the Shepherd and his flock. We are the branches and we are connected to Jesus, the vine that brings life.

How do we participate in the "pruning" and fruit bearing? Simply, by avoiding the temptations that cause us to be removed from the vine. We also need to recognize the hardships and sufferings that come our way which can actually move us along our spiritual journey. It is a paradox of life that when our bodies are enjoying the distracting pleasures of life, our spirits are often the farthest from a loving trust in God. And conversely, the more we are in distress, the closer we come to a dependence on God.

Recently I was washing grapes for my guests when I was awed by the most bountiful cluster of well-rounded grapes. I had to pause and draw attention to the beautiful fruit on that vine. Our wish should be that God, the vinedresser, will pause from his labors when he beholds us and say: "Look at the beautiful fruit that comes from this vine!"

The best way to continue to bear fruit is to be in the church, which is the Body of Christ on earth—Christ is the vine, we are the branches. When Scripture talks about us human beings as the Body of Christ (1 Corinthians 12:27), it seems a difficult concept to comprehend. Saint Paul does not say to his fellow Christians, "You are like the Body of Christ," he says, "You are the Body of Christ." What does that mean? Saint Augustine, in a homily to Christians who were about to receive the Eucharist for the first time, put it this way: "You ought to know that what you will receive, what you ought to receive daily, the bread that you see upon the altar which has been sanctified by the Word of God, is the Body of Christ. The cup, or more accurately what the cup contains, sanctified by the Word of God, is the blood of Christ. By these, the bread and wine, Christ wanted to entrust us with his body and blood which he shed for the forgiveness of our sins. If you receive this well, you are what you receive." In the Christian community, in a real sense, we are the hands and feet of Christ. All of us, whatever our talents, can contribute to making this world a better place, helping God's Kingdom to come to fruition.

How are we, in essence, Christ on earth? When we are there for a dying sister or brother, we are Christ; when we give so much as a drink of cold water, we are Christ; when we respect the person and dignity of a fellow human being, we respect Christ's presence in that person; when we visit a shut-in, we are Christ; and when we struggle for social justice against an unwieldy bureaucracy, we are Christ. Jesus is truly present in our world today. The most concrete way we see him is in the community of believers, the church, who live out his mandate and who lay down their lives in dedication to their fellow man. We do not have to look far for examples. Christ is in the loving surrender of a spouse in marriage; he is in a sacrificing father or mother; he is in a single person working for others; he is in the celibate who has dedicated his or her life in poverty, chastity and obedience; he is in an obedient child, a selfless student, or a helping hand. Where love is, there God is also: "If we love one another, God lives in us" (1 John: 4:12).

SITTING NEXT TO THE CHAFF

One of the struggles we face today is getting along with each other so we can be the Body of Christ on earth. Some abandon church because of the discord that is too often a part of our normal associations with each other; others abandon church because they find it irrelevant. Thornton Wilder in his play *Our Town* says: "Wherever you come near the human race, there's layers and layers of nonsense." He says further that humans "…move about in a cloud of ignorance…always at the mercy of one self-centered passion or another." Wilder seems to have an extraordinary grasp of the frailty of human nature. As adults we are keenly aware of the shortcomings of our neighbors and associates. Every community has its north against south, east against west, "just" against "sinner;" and we know which side we are on.

Church groups are not exempt—clergy and flock alike. That person sitting next to you, the one you really can't stand, is she the chaff and you are the wheat? Isn't it uncomfortable sitting next to that guy? Don't ask me to shake his hand. Is anyone exempt from this human nature? God put us on this earth with our weaknesses and passions, and lets us struggle toward the eternal kingdom. But we are not left as orphans. Christ sent the Holy Spirit to give us the wisdom to love our neighbor. Perhaps we need to pray more for the power to discern the truth. Perhaps we need to pray more for our neighbor. The Lord of the harvest will let all grow together until the harvest is ready. We are in for a big surprise come judgment day. That person we least can stand, he or she may be there to welcome us into the Kingdom. For sure, we can only be welcome in God's Kingdom if we can sit beside those we know and who know us.

Let me illustrate one way we can build community in our normal association as church. Recently I was privy to an exchange of smiles between two people. Innocent it was. One of the two was a lady who was over thirty, and the other was a youth about seventeen. What made this situation unique was that the event took place in church, during a solemn liturgy. The lad was a Mass server at the altar and the lady was a member of the choir. I saw him smile, and I was puzzled because I knew few if any of his friends were present at the service. When I glanced to where he was looking, I could see the only other person who was smiling.

Then I had a realization. The smile by the lady was saying, "Thank you! We appreciate the fact that you are present and serving in this parish community. We are happy to have you here." His smile was saying, "You're welcome. And thanks for making this more enjoyable." I have a feeling if there were more smiles and thank-yous, there would be more young people in church.

The lack of attendance of young people in some of our churches today presents a problem. How are we to understand God's plan in this? Thomas Beaudoin in *Virtual Faith: The Irreverent Spiritual Quest of Generation X* suggests that youth today find God in a different way. Beaudoin describes playing lead guitar and riding the low notes or stomping through a syncopated rumble as a spiritual experience: "We move our bodies and souls in harmony with the music, which is in harmony with the Spirit of God." Sounds like religion? Beaudoin explains in part why many younger people, by and large, do not frequent church services. Their cynicism, he suggests, may be related to the droll music, the outdated technology, retrograde social teaching and a hostile or indifferent attitude toward popular culture.

It is too true! Can you name many churches that have a sound system as good as or as expensive as the "music machines" many young people possess? And the music you hear in church on Sunday morning is often not lively enough for those under fifty.

As to the popularity of the social teachings of mainline Christian churches? Young people can sense if the older adults in a community stand for anything. Moral clarity is essential. Our lives should be sacramental—standing as a clear sign of what we believe in. And as to popular culture? It is easy to take the moral high road and condemn rather than understand. Again, we need to present values that challenge those seen in movies and on TV. Looking back at our parents and grandparents we can see how this works and how it should work. I am still striving to live the values and ideals exemplified in the lives of my mother and father. There is so much we can do to make sure our children and grandchildren feel the same way.

One thing we need much more of is pure and simple joy. Have you ever been around truly joy-filled people? I know a priest who is so filled with the utter joy of Christ that he gets silly beyond words. At family gatherings he can't speak out an even sentence. He is too silly. I know, because I've swapped jokes with him—I mean his list for mine! I know he gets his energy from the Lord. Saint Dominic used to labor through long days at his task of preaching to and discussing the gospel with heretics. And at night he would want only one reward, to be in the presence of the Blessed Sacrament, pouring out his soul in love to Jesus. He would lean his head against the altar and rest a little, then he would converse with Jesus. In the morning when he celebrated Mass, his body was raised in the air in ecstasy. There was no doubt about where he got his energy.

You and I have enough trouble dragging ourselves out of bed and to work some mornings, even after six or eight hours of sleep. If we had a little more real joy in our lives, the kind that spills over to others, our days would be less tiring. Jesus' habitual greeting to the disciples he appeared to after his Resurrection was: "Peace be with you!" (Luke 24:37). The effect he had on his followers was that they were "filled with awe and great joy" and ran to tell others, like the holy women at the tomb (Matthew 28:8). We are still in the post-Resurrection time and our lives should reflect the same urgent joy to others.

ECUMENICAL FISH STORY

When you compare the tales of a fisherman and a golfer, you may be amazed at the ardent lengths they will go to tell their story. The golfer uses two fingers on one hand to indicate how close he came to that hole in one, whereas the fisherman uses both hands and a good deal of arm to express how big was the one that got away. Though there appears to be a great contrast in their stories, there is also a significant similarity.

The spread of Christianity in a sense began with the biggest fish story of all. In Luke 5:4–8 we read how Jesus asks Simon Peter to cast his net one more time. Peter says, "We have worked all night long, but caught nothing. Yet if you say so, I will let down the nets." They catch such a large number of fish that their nets begin to tear. Jesus says to them: "…from now on you will be catching people," and they leave their boats to follow him.

"Fishers of men" and "the nets are full to breaking" might describe the followers of Christ today. There is one "catch" though. Each January we complete another "Ecumenical Week" which asks us to focus on the unity of all Christian faiths. In the abundance of the harvest we must not lose sight of the net and the Master Fisherman. That is what ties us together as pilgrims on the true path. At the same time an embarrassment of Christian unity today is the division that we find among even the mainline churches. We need to pray for and work for a happy ending to our fish story. Our understanding of the Body of Christ must be based on the words of Christ himself on the night before his death. In John 17:20–21 Jesus prays for his followers:

> I ask…that they may all be one. As you, Father, are
> in me and I am in you, may they also be in us, so that
> the world may believe that you have sent me.

Christianity generally is getting a good grade in passing on the message of Christ. Recently I looked over the congregation at Sunday morning worship and reflected on the success of Christianity in our town and in our world. We are doing a good job of passing on the Word to our families and our communities, and there is evidence of Christian values in our civilization and in its philosophies.

The question is, of course, why are we not more conscious of what we are doing, and could we do a better job? How did Christianity even survive the shameful death of its founder and the scattering, in fear, of his followers? The answer is simply that the movement is guided by God and the power of the Holy Spirit. Nothing can stop that. John the Baptist is an excellent example of the Lord's plan in action. Before he was born, he reacted to Christ's presence when Mary visited her cousin Elizabeth. At Mary's greeting, John leaped in his mother's womb (Luke 1:41). John went on to do God's will by prophesying about and pointing the way to Jesus. There was no vanity in John. He gave his life so Jesus would "increase" and he "decrease." Today, fully one-third of the people on earth are Christian.

Trusting in God and placing ourselves at his disposal is the best we can do. In Isaiah 55:11 God says, "so shall my word be that goes out from my mouth; / it shall not return to me empty, / but it shall accomplish that which I purpose, / and succeed in the thing for which I sent it." We are instruments of the Lord in more ways than we realize. Like John the Baptist we do give witness when we proclaim the Word. That family decision to return to worship on Sunday mornings, that prayer for the Chechens in Grozny, the acts of charity to a family member or neighbor, or simply being a witness to the world that Christ is alive and working among us—all these are ways that we are doing a good job working for the Kingdom of God. Once in a while we need to realize what we are all about and rejoice greatly, praising Jesus who has redeemed us and found us worth dying for.

I would like to conclude this chapter with a lighter side look at the "Top Ten Reasons for Going to Church." Recently I was in a whimsical mood as I watched David Letterman, and I thought about what the top ten reasons for going to church might be. I didn't finish ten, but among the list would be "to see what people are wearing," "so people don't talk about us," and perhaps the number one reason might be "so the Lord will recognize us when they carry us in that final time."

On a more serious note, there are fundamental principles that we can accept, and then going to church is natural and easy. The first principle we need to accept is that Jesus died for our sins—past, present and future. His love redeems us, forgives us and has bought and paid for us. In this *love* relationship we want to and need to praise him, thank him and just "abide" in him. A second fundamental principle is that our greatest sin is our failure to love. If we truly love God, that alone would negate our sinful inclinations. If we love our neighbors, we will not harm them, envy them or say nasty things about them. The greatest law Jesus gave us is twofold: to love God above all, and to love our neighbor as ourselves. It is simple.

A pharmacy ethicist said in a speech: "People don't care how much you know until they know how much you care." An application of this saying might suggest that if we knew how much Jesus cares for us, we would be more concerned about getting to know him. We would join the community (the church) he set up for us, and we would listen to his word, praise him and enjoy his favor on a regular basis.

CHAPTER SEVEN

The Holy Spirit

The greatest gift of all is the hope of divine life through the Spirit. Too often we lose sight of that hope. In the movie *The Apostle*, a preacher played by Robert Duvall talks directly to God at a desperate time in his life. His wife has broken up their marriage and has taken his church away from him. He is very direct with God: "Blow this pain out of me! Give me peace. I'm confused. I'm mad! I love you Lord, but I'm mad at you." He admits his sinful nature: "I know I'm a sinner, a womanizer...but I'm your servant. What should I do? I always call you Jesus. You always call me son."

Now that's a beautiful relationship with God. The character Sonny never gives up hope. He talks directly with God, like Jacob wrestling all night with God. But he never loses sight of his vision of the eternal. We need to talk directly with God every day. It's called prayer. Sonny's life is grounded in the sure knowledge that one day he will be on that jetliner to heaven. He believes in the Good News: "Someday I'm going to get on that plane, on that runway to the sky. I'm not going to Jackson, Mississippi; I'm not going to Chicago, Illinois; I'm not going to Paris, France. I'm going yonder to heaven. Get out of the way moon. Get out of the way stars. I'm going on that runway to heaven."

We need to be a little more direct with our spiritual lives. There has to be an interaction with God every day. When "dark times" come upon us, we need to say, like Sonny: "Get behind me Satan." The real joy of life is when we are on the path to that "runway in the sky." And that is accomplished when we are plugged in to the Holy Spirit on a daily basis.

Do you remember fear of the darkness as a child? Often it would keep me from sleep. On the farm where I grew up it was very dark before electricity came to the area in 1955. Coyotes would howl, and the consoling sound of our collie dog barking in the night gave me a little security. But an unusual sound in the dark could still paralyze me with fear. Ultimately the real security came when I trusted in supernatural powers. My guardian angel would protect me. "The force" of God was in my bedroom. It also helped that I shared the room (and the bed) with some older brothers.

The real security in my childhood came from the presence of loving parents who had power over the dark. My father could strike a match and its light in his hand dispelled the black night. The love and presence of my parents helped to push back the fears of night and death. The death of a cousin or a neighbor would cause real fear of the dark to return. For a short time I could practically see ghosts and evil forces in the pitch black of the night. Real fear had returned. I would struggle at the philosophic level until some equilibrium could again be established.

Finding security as an adult is much easier. "Rejoice and believe the Good News." To have the sense of peace of a child sleeping in the night, we need to have faith in the power of Jesus over death. Life and death are in God's loving hands. The Father has the Light of our lives in his hands. Its light pushes back the black night forever. The Father of Light has enlightened our minds by the outpouring of His Spirit. It is no accident that the Holy Spirit on Pentecost was manifested in tongues of fire, expressing both *light* and *energy*. That light has forever dispelled the fear of the night and is energizing us to dream dreams and see visions.

Saint Peter says that when the Holy Spirit is poured out, "…your sons and daughters shall prophesy, and your young men shall see visions, and your old men shall dream dreams" (Acts 2:17). Have you seen a vision lately? (The thing that worries me is that I'm starting to dream…and that would make me…?)

Pentecost, the season focusing on the Holy Spirit, follows Easter. My vision (or dream) this year has to do with *light* in our world. All of us can picture that first night in the Bethlehem countryside when Light dawned and the star shone above the manger. The heavens were opened and angels were heard singing. "The people who walked in darkness / have seen a great light; / those who lived in the land of deep darkness— / on them light has shined" (Isaiah 9:2).

A FIRE OF LOVE

One thrill I would wish for everyone is to experience the fire of love that is the Holy Spirit alive in our world today. We have all seen individuals aflame with a zeal that is undeniable as it is contagious. "What gas do they operate on?" we ask.

Jesus brought the fire of divine love to earth. "I came to bring fire to the earth, and how I wish it were already kindled!" (Luke 12:49). We know that the Holy Spirit came down on the disciples at Pentecost in flames of fire. That same fire is in baptized Christians, and that same mandate is passed on to us, "Go and make disciples of all nations." In our lives we need to recognize what comes from the Spirit and let it guide our decisions and directions. I will share a couple of examples of what I mean.

A few years ago when the Canora Council of Churches was meeting to plan Church Unity Week, our meeting bogged down when we tried to put volunteers to the task of carrying out our plans. Reverend Allan Witan, who was chairing the meeting, called a halt and asked us to reflect in prayer. I was moved to call aloud to the Holy Spirit to "enkindle in us the fire" of his love, to "send forth" his spirit and to renew us and give us wisdom. The meeting continued after a few more moments of silent reflection. Suddenly there were volunteers and there was action. Clearly, there was new energy that had not been at the meeting earlier.

Occasionally when I am preparing these articles I get a definite indication that the inspiration does not come from my limited knowledge and wisdom. Recently I had an article all typed and ready to e-mail. I did a final check and noticed a turn of a phrase that was meant to appeal to a fringe group in our society. I suddenly realized it would offend and alienate rather than invite. And just this past week I spent much of one day struggling to write an article while fighting a headache. I "sort of" completed it. The next morning I sat at my keyboard and with a few deft switches of phrases and "quick inspirations" I realized what it was the Spirit wanted me to say.

I have seen the work of the Spirit in my younger brother Ron. I remember growing up with him on a humble farm ten miles from the hamlet of Cactus Lake. When a coyote came along it was an event! After reading some of his articles and books I eventually got over my initial reaction: "Where is he getting all this wisdom?" As his older brother I used to think myself superior to him, naturally. Simply put, the Holy Spirit is at work in a special way that allows him and us (you and me) to touch peoples' hearts.

Cardinal Newman said that God had a special task for him to do that he did not have for anyone else. You and I have a special role to play in our situation in life. No one else can do the job that is ours alone. No one else is in our shoes. It is not such a bad job, to work for a carpenter's son.

How do we find that "fire of love" that is the Spirit alive in our world today? One day as I sat here writing, the wind was rippling through the leaves outside my window. I was struck by the manifestation of the Holy Spirit through wind on that first Pentecost. The symbols used by God to represent the Spirit are wind, fire and breath. These are powerful symbols.

Breath we know is precious. Watching an asthmatic struggling to breathe recently brought that home to me. But breath also symbolizes the Spirit of God the Father. We can easily understand the natural power of fire. And metaphorically we know we can catch the fire of the Spirit to motivate our lives. Wind is something of a metaphysical reality. In *Who Has Seen The Wind,* W. O. Mitchell used the wind to represent the power of God. Wind was present at that first Pentecost.

How and where do we find the Holy Spirit today? A good place to start is in the church, which was born on that first Pentecost. What do we find in the church? One of the functions of the church is worship or liturgy. As a child I learned that liturgical prayer is more powerful because it involves Christ praying through his church. The purpose of all liturgy is to give glory to God: Father, Son and Holy Spirit. In simpler terms, think of the joy of the Creator in seeing the full realization of goodness in his creatures. Our highest role as creatures is to offer worship to and share a oneness with our Creator.

The church prays, works and lives through the power of the Holy Spirit. The Holy Spirit renews and enlivens the effective work of the church—to bring the Good News to all nations. It is not a mistake that God chose Pentecost, fifty days after Easter, to manifest the work of the Holy Spirit, and to breathe life into his church. Pentecost originally was a Jewish harvest festival celebrated fifty days after the Passover. Harvest is a rich metaphor for the work of the church. "The harvest is plentiful, but the laborers are few" (Matthew 9:37).

So if we are not in touch with the Holy Spirit in our daily lives, going to church might be the first step in finding the Holy Spirit in today's world. If we never make the time or take time to be with the Lord, nothing spiritual can happen in our lives. In 1 John 2:20 Jesus tells his disciples they have been "anointed" by the Holy One and received "knowledge," one of the fruits of the Spirit. Jesus here refers to the anointing with chrism, which in the Old Testament symbolized the Spirit or Breath of Yahweh (God the Father). The richness of this anointing has been carried on in the Christian churches to this day.

Ultimately, what does the Holy Spirit do in our lives? In Galatians 5:22 we read that the Spirit brings: "…love, joy, peace, patience, kindness, generosity, faithfulness, gentleness, and self-control." Elsewhere in Isaiah 11 we read of the gifts that come through the breath of God: wisdom and insight, counsel and power, knowledge and fear of God. When Jesus left this earth to go to the Father, he left with us the Spirit that renews and enlivens us and all creation. The Ascension actually made it possible for him to be much closer to us. Suppose Christ were still on earth in human form. How close would we, personally, feel to him if he were in Palestine, or Rome, or Brazil? He is in fact much closer to us than that. His love touches our hearts daily as we strive to love others and are forgiven for our frequent lapses into imperfection. We have the sense of daily communion with a personal God. He is there like a traveling companion when things are tough.

What does Jesus do in heaven? A good question! Actually, in heaven Jesus continues his work on earth. Paradoxically, on earth he did the work of his Father in heaven. The answer to the paradox is that Jesus came here to make earth more like heaven: "Thy Kingdom come, Thy will be done on earth as it is in heaven!" Jesus is still with us. The best of this world, our closeness to each other in our families and in our communities, is the beginning of heaven. Death will not be so much an ending of the things of this world as heaven will be a continuation of the best of this life. A realization of this truth helps us to know we are on the right path in our journey to the Father.

What are we to do on earth as we wait for Jesus to return? On the Feast of the Ascension, which is celebrated forty days after Easter, we read about how the men of Galilee stood around after Christ ascended, gazing up to heaven. An angel appeared and said, "Men of Galilee, why do you stand looking up toward heaven? This Jesus...will come in the same way as you saw him go into heaven (Acts 1:11)." If we sidestep the masculine tone of the Gospel, the real message is: "Men and women of Canora, why do you stand here looking up to heaven? Jesus will come again. Your job is to go out there and work for the kingdom."

It is easy to do our task when there is a romantic thrill of travel or a new job involved. But what about when it means working hard at our everyday, mundane, ordinary *work*? Jesus tells us to be faithful in the little things, to do our part. The eleven who stood looking up to heaven were ordinary enough people like us. Some, because of their opportunity, were even greater sinners (remember Peter's betrayal). Yet with the power of the Holy Spirit they accomplished mightily!

In Mark 16:15–20 Jesus commissions us to go into the world and minister. Signs and wonders will accompany us and, with God's grace, we will cast out demons (some in our own lives). We will lay our hands on the sick and they will recover. In fact we do bring solace and comfort to the sick to help relieve their pain and anguish. How many times has a parent worked miracles for a child's scraped knee? Sometimes it was by applying a simple Band-Aid and a little tenderness.

We can work wonders in our ordinary, workaday relationships.

Love and care can do so much more than a pill or injection to help bring about healing of the Spirit and soul. So, men and women of Canora, do not stand around looking up at the heavens, waiting for the Second Coming. This Jesus whom you have seen ascend will come in the same way you have seen him go into heaven.

Consider our calling to cooperate with the Spirit as we live our daily lives. "Listen to me, O coastlands, / pay attention, you peoples from far away! / The Lord called me before I was born, / while I was in my mother's womb he named me" (Isaiah 49:1). How easy it is for us to apply these words to John the Baptist, whose feast we celebrate June 24. The liturgy of the day includes the above reading, which continues: "He made my mouth like a sharp sword, in the shadow of his hand he hid me; he made me a polished arrow, in his quiver he hid me away." I repeat, how easy it is to apply these words to Isaiah or John the Baptist. But they apply with equal force to you and to me. We are called to be a "light to the nations, / that my [the Lord's] salvation may reach to the end of the earth" (Isaiah 49:6).

Recently I tuned in to a TV program that talked about the contributions of Pierre Trudeau to world history. I mused about that. What is our contribution to the events of salvation history? The good we engender in the world may well be more significant than the political contributions of many a statesman. We cannot be Christians and remain silent or fearful. The message of Christ must be shouted out to others, as John the Baptist did and as Isaiah did. We are called to fearless evangelization—we are to "proclaim from the housetops" what we hear whispered in silence (Matthew 10:27).

Most of us cringe at the thought of professing our faith openly. We are shy about saying a prayer before we eat in a restaurant. Maybe we hesitate to tell our friends at the party Saturday night that we are going to church Sunday morning. We are those who "whisper" our beliefs rather than "shout" them from the housetops. What are we lacking? The Spirit can make us bold. The Holy Spirit can transform and empower us. We must reflect in silence and let the Spirit address our inner beings. In time we will grow bolder and more able to proclaim the truth.

The truth is that each one of us is as special as the infant John the Baptist was, kicking in his mother Elizabeth's womb. God says to us: "You are my servant…in whom I will be glorified…I will give you as a light to the nations" (Isaiah 49:3–6). Even Saint Paul recognizes this when he says, "God…had set me apart before I was born" (Galatians 1:15).

I would like to conclude this chapter with some anecdotal reflection of how the Spirit is found in our world today. Two little boys dug a hole and were ready to bury their dead pup. They stood around not knowing what to say. A third boy came along and offered to perform the necessary ritual. He took the pup and said, "In the name of the father, and of the son, and in the hole he goes." Wouldn't it be nice if we had the instant "high speed" connection to the God we need?

Recently I attended a church service in an inner-city parish that was populated largely by seniors. I thought I had made a mistake when a "senior" clergy appeared and informed us he was replacing another priest who was in ill health. The feast we were celebrating was Holy Trinity Sunday, and I wondered what kind of a reflection we would hear.

The Spirit is a surprise, and is very much alive and active in our churches today. The homilist introduced his theme with a story about a kindergarten substitute teacher who at the end of the day helped a boy dress to catch the bus. After she helped put on the boy's boots he said, "These boots are on the wrong feet." Patiently the teacher changed the boots. "They're not my boots," the boy said. She took them off again. "They're my brother's," said the boy. "Mom makes me wear them." After patiently putting on the boots one more time, the teacher asked, "Where are your mittens?" "I put them in the toes of the boots," said the boy.

The point of the story was that if a kindergarten child can present such a mystery to a teacher, why should we not be puzzled by the complexities of three persons in one God? I mused about this. Just what is the reason for three persons in the Trinity? I am reminded of a story about a little girl who was crying during a violent thunderstorm. Her mother tried to comfort her, "Don't cry. God will look after you." "But Mommy, I want a God with skin on!" said the little girl.

We need a God that we can relate to at the human level. That is the gift of Jesus, a God enfleshed in our form. God the *Son* we can relate to. And not only that, Christ came to reveal the love of the Father to us. We need a Father who puts us in awe, a Father who created us and everything else, a Father who is a planner and architect of the universe; yet a loving parent we can relate to as sons and daughters (through Baptism).

The Holy Spirit is more real in our world than perhaps the Father and the Son. When Jesus left he said he would send the Spirit who would teach us all things: "You will receive power when the Spirit comes on you, and then you will be my witnesses...to the ends of the earth" (Acts 1:8).

The Holy Spirit is our high-speed connection to the Father and the Son. In an instant the Spirit will inspire us, lead us, guide us and even turn a liturgical celebration in a graying inner-city church into a spiritual experience. We need to be tuned in to the workings of the Trinity if we want to be high-tech Christians, metaphorically, in a high-tech spirituality.

CHAPTER EIGHT

Prayer

Many of my readers have seen the picture of the praying hands, and some will remember the story. I revisited this masterpiece recently and it still brings a tear to my eye.

In fifteenth-century Nuremberg, in a tiny village, lived a goldsmith who had eighteen children. Despite his efforts working eighteen hours a day he could not provide for the full education of his children. Two brothers decided they would flip a coin to see which one would work to help the other through art school. Then they would reverse the process. Albert lost, and Albrecht Dürer quickly became famous for his etchings, woodcuts and oils. At a ceremonial supper Albrecht now offered to send his brother through art school. "No...no...no...no," sobbed Albert aloud, tears streaming down his cheeks. "It is too late for me. Look...what four years in the mines have done to my hands! The bones in every finger have been smashed at least once...I have arthritis...I cannot hold a glass to return your toast." Albrecht paid the dearest tribute to his brother's sacrifice by drawing those hands with palms together and fingers stretched skyward. The world named his work "The Praying Hands."

As I reflected on the powerful message in this story I realized I had witnessed similar sacrifice and love in twentieth-century North America. I can still see my father's roughened hands with a finger missing here and a depression there where a bone was absent. He and my mother raised sixteen children on a dry-land farm. Chronicling the sacrifices involved in nurturing and educating those children would fill a sizeable volume.

My parents' hands are still very much alive to me today, more than thirty years after their deaths. The hours, weeks, months and years of my mother's cooking, sewing, washing, knitting, stitching and praying are still bearing fruit in the extended family that carries on the same traditions of caring and sacrifice. My father's hands as well, like the hands of Christ stretched out and pierced, brought a love to our world that is not bound by time and place, but in a mystical sense continues to give to us.

Our hands today, when they are not folded, with palms together and their fingers stretched skyward, are at work loving God's kingdom into reality. When you reach out and touch someone, help someone, your hands are the hands of Christ still at work on earth. When parents care for their children, when lovers touch, God's love is still communicated with a sweet mystery that somehow makes up for the calluses and blisters, for the scars and the scrapes.

DAILY PRAYER

In one of his essays humorist Eric Nichol translates our Canadian national motto from Latin into English: "*a mare usque ad mare*" (literally, "from sea to sea") becomes "a little water with your wine." In the liturgical ritual of the Mass as it is celebrated in the Catholic church, a little water is added to the wine to represent the humanity of Christ. Though he was Divine, yet he was human. In our daily lives we should strive to always have a little wine with our water. But spirituality is more than just prayer. Prayer is not enough. We also need to share pierogies on occasion. As Saint James said, "Charity without works is dead." We must always strive to be a visible sign, to do good works that are tangible in a human way.

For some time now I have been the happy recipient of regular and faithful prayer from a gracious lady who has sort of adopted me in a spiritual sense. Thanks to the prayers of her and others, I sense the Holy Spirit working through me as I strive to find time and inspiration to write spiritual reflections during my busy schedule. I know that I owe much to the prayers of this lady and others who pray for this particular mission of spreading the Good News. On occasion, also, my family and I have been the happy recipients of some pierogies (or other treats) that have been sent with the same love as the prayers. Prayers for the spirit, pierogies for the body! Thank you!

In our world the corporal works of mercy are so desperately needed. It is easier to believe in a God that we cannot see if we witness love and service in a way that we can see. We want something tangible, something we can sense. Let me illustrate. The story is told of a man conversing with God:

> "Is it true that to you time is not the same as it is to us, that a million years can seem like a second?"
>
> "Yes."
>
> "It true that you are all powerful and can do anything?"
>
> "Yes."
>
> "You could, for example, make me a millionaire?"
>
> "Yes."
>
> "OK, God, can you please make me a millionaire."
>
> "OK, just a second."

There is a deep lesson in this story. We want things now! We want results, or we cry out, "Where are you God?" How do we reach a patient understanding of the ways of God?

Two examples come to mind. In Job 7:1–7 we read about our "hard service on earth." Our days are like that of a laborer who longs for the shade and looks for the wages. Job says, "...so I am allotted months of emptiness, and nights of misery...my eye will never again see good." And Job was famous for his patience. We've all been there, in the realm of despair.

A second example gives us more hope. Simeon spent years waiting for the messiah to come. Day after day he came to the temple. Boy those days can sometimes drag in our lives. Yet Simeon never gave up hope. He listened patiently for the Holy Spirit, and the years passed, day by slow day. Finally one day a baby was brought to the temple to be consecrated to the Lord according to the custom. Then Simeon took the child in his arms and, recognizing the Lord, said, "Master, now you are dismissing your servant in peace...for my eyes have seen your

salvation, which you have prepared in the presence of all peoples"
(Luke 2:29–31).

Jesus himself waited for thirty years until he started his public
life and went forth to proclaim the Kingdom to all. You and I need to
recognize the opportunity in our years of waiting for the Spirit in our
lives. Finally, we reach the moment when we recognize Jesus and say,
"It is He!"

Where are you God? The answer has been given to us by Simeon
and by Jesus. God sent his son to *reveal* the Kingdom to us. The waiting is over. We have the church and Scripture to provide answers. Our
lives should be richer than that of Job and Simeon, who both illustrate
a prayerful patience we can learn from. But in our secular world we
find distraction easier than prayer.

How many times did you think of God yesterday? A headline in a
daily paper said: "Board Supports Removing the Lord's Prayer." What
is wrong with daily spiritual reminders, even if they are from another
creed? I was concerned recently about whether or not my children are
in touch with God on a daily basis. Do families still say grace before
meals? Is there still family prayer? Morning and night prayer?

In Romans 8:22–23 Saint Paul says: "We know that the whole
creation has been groaning in labor pains until now; not only creation,
but we ourselves, who have the first fruits of the Spirit, groan inwardly
while we wait for adoption, the redemption of our bodies." In a sense
it is our bodies that do most of the groaning. With age and illness and
the suffering to which our flesh is heir, we are reminded that our bodies, too, need eternal redemption. We look forward to a final resurrection when all pain will be gone and we will get our bodies back in
spectacular health and vigor. I like to imagine what it will be like
when we can pass through walls. Or imagine the body of a great ath-
lete or a loved one who has wasted away with illness being fully
restored to physical perfection.

In a purely spiritual way, we know the beauty of God's plan of salvation. Our spirits groan for birth, a birth as sons and daughters of
God. Real joy is experienced in this oneness with the Lord and with

each other. Sin is a dark tunnel. Sin makes us addicts, wallowing in slavery. Who would not rather be free?

And so we groan for birth. We share the universal hunger of our fellow man. From primitive times to the present we have been searching, seeking the Divine. There is something in our very nature that does not want to be swallowed up in an aimless secular existence. There is a great merit in the discipline of prayer patterns and surrounding ourselves with signs and reminders of a brighter future in eternity.

One formula prayer we are all familiar with and which deserves individual reflection is the Lord's Prayer. One reflection on this prayer begins: "Our Father, who art in heaven..."

"Yes?"

"Don't interrupt me. I'm praying..." So goes an imaginary discussion in the "Our Father" skit in which God speaks to a child who is rattling off a formula prayer. In the ensuing dialogue we see some of the implications of this tremendous prayer. The Father also points out as the child is asking for "daily bread": "You need to cut out some of that bread. You're overweight as it is." But the lesson gets more profound as the child tries to rattle through part of the prayer: "Forgive us our trespassesasweforgivethosewhotresspassagainstus..." "What about Linda?" God asks.

In Matthew's version, 6:7–14, Jesus says, "And forgive our debts, as we also have forgiven our debtors." This is fairly demanding. We cannot just promise to forgive others, but we will receive forgiveness only as we have already forgiven others. Another implication spelled out in the "Our Father" skit has to do with praying for God's Kingdom to come on earth. The Father asks: "What are you doing about it?"

One of my fondest memories of this great prayer involves this particular theme of working for the Kingdom. Father Charles Gibney was a pastor in Canora several years back. I remember him standing with arms outstretched, joining in singing the Lord's Prayer. Because of his age and health, he had a condition that caused his fingers to involuntarily gesture in much the same way as one would beckon when inviting someone to come and join him. To me, Father Charles was standing there with arms outstretched between heaven and earth, beckoning all to come to the Great Banquet Feast. Father Charles has since joined that feast, but his invitation and his gesture still stands. No one took his pastoral duties more seriously. His compassion for reconciliation was what the Lord's Prayer is all about.

Another thought that strikes me in the Lord's Prayer has to do with the opening lines. When we say "Our Father" we are acknowledging an intimate relationship with God. At a more profound level, this acknowledgement is reciprocal. Not only *is* God our Father, we *are* his sons and daughters. When God looks at us he sees all the promise and talents he has given us. I know what it is like to look at my children and see talent and promise that they may not even be aware of yet. Is our heavenly Father's vision of us less profound?

A French proverb says: "To know all is to forgive all." If only we could see ourselves as our heavenly Father sees us! We are more than we appear. We see our sins; God sees our Spirit. Here is where real trust comes in. We need to have faith in ourselves as God's creation. As we pray for God's Kingdom to come, for our daily bread, for forgiveness and for protection, we need to trust a little more. We need to pour ourselves out working for the Kingdom to come, for forgiveness and reconciliation, as Father Charles Gibney did. The Lord's Prayer is a dynamic prayer, meant to move us to life.

Our prayers can be powerful weapons against the greatest wrongs in the world. In Revelation 5:8 John sees our prayers offered before God as a bowl full of incense placed before the Lord. Through prayer we can stop ethnic cleansing, famine and war. How do we do this?

First, we do not pray alone. In Hebrews 7 we read that Christ's priesthood is eternal, "...he is able for all time to save those who approach God through him." Christ said if we ask the Father for anything in his name, the Father will answer our prayer. We do not need to feel helpless when the world overwhelms us, since we do not pray alone. Second, the Holy Spirit intercedes for us, taking our prayers directly to God, even giving us the words to say: "For we do not know to pray as we ought, but that very Spirit intercedes with sighs too deep for words. And God, who searches the heart, knows what is the mind of the Spirit." (Romans 8:26).

Part of the mystery of prayer is learning to listen to God. Recently I overheard part of a talk show about a celebrity. In essence the host was saying that the experience of meeting with this person of few words was refreshing. It was a joy just to be in his or her company. We can all relate to the situation of being with a significant other whom we love and respect; a grandparent, for example. I remember as a child visiting my German-speaking grandmother. I was not very fluent with the language and felt awkward and unworthy. But I realized words were not really so important. Just sitting in her presence and sharing the moment was good for both of us and brought immeasurable and inexpressible joy.

This can happen in our communion with God. We need merely be present, enjoying the moment. We do not have to be saying the right words or speaking the right language. We can trust God's perception of the situation. We need only to create the right disposition in our hearts for a joyful and precious meeting with God. I realize it is an unfair analogy to compare a visit with God to a visit with Grandmother. God loves us much more.

There is a story from the Internet that perhaps best illustrates how we can commune with God and not worry about saying the right words:

> A man's daughter had asked the local minister to come and pray with her father. When the minister arrived, he found the man lying in bed with his head propped up on two pillows. An empty chair sat beside his bed. The minister assumed that the old fellow had been informed of his visit.
> "I guess you were expecting me," he said.
> "No, who are you?" said the father.
> The minister told him his name and then remarked, "I see the empty chair; I figured you knew I was going to show up."

"Oh yeah, the chair," said the bedridden man. "Would you mind closing the door?"

Puzzled, the minister shut the door. "I have never told anyone this, not even my daughter," said the man. "But all of my life I have never known how to pray. At church I used to hear the pastor talk about prayer, but it went right over my head. I abandoned any attempt at prayer," the old man continued, "until one day four years ago my best friend said to me, 'Johnny, prayer is just a simple matter of having a conversation with Jesus. Here is what I suggest. Sit down in a chair; place an empty chair in front of you, and in faith see Jesus on the chair. It's not spooky because he promised: "I'll be with you always." Then just speak to him in the same way you're doing with me right now.'

"So, I tried it and I've liked it so much that I do it a couple of hours every day. I'm careful though. If my daughter saw me talking to an empty chair, she'd either have a nervous breakdown or send me off to the funny farm."

The minister was deeply moved by the story and encouraged the old man to continue on the journey. Then he prayed with him, anointed him with oil, and returned to the church.

Two nights later the daughter called to tell the minister that her daddy had died that afternoon. "Did he die in peace?" he asked.

"Yes, when I left the house about two o'clock, he called me over to his bedside, told me he loved me and kissed me on the cheek. When I got back from the store an hour later, I found him dead. But there was something strange about his death. Apparently, just before Daddy died, he leaned over and rested his head on the chair beside the bed. What do you make of that?"

The minister wiped a tear from his eye and said, "I wish we could all go like that!"

Ultimately we need to get our lives "on side" with Christ's sacrifice. The great secret of sainthood is to unite our spirits to the will of Christ. We are still sinners, but God can make a "silk purse" out of our "sow's ear." The spirit of our lives must be directed toward heaven and the will of the Father. In this way our lives will be a prayer, even when we don't know the words, and God can use us. We do not have to spend hours on our knees every day. We do simply have to offer our lives as instruments of God. Our will has to belong to God so that collectively Christ is alive in this world in his followers. Then everything we do, think and say will ultimately reflect Christ.

IN THE NAME OF JESUS

We need to pray in the name of Jesus. A comedian on radio once referred to the story of Moses and the burning bush. God told Moses to take off his shoes because the ground was holy. The comedian added that as Moses approached in his bare feet on the hot ground, we find the first reference to Jesus Christ in the Old Testament. Irreverent, yes, but also funny. The point is that you and I have heard about Jesus Christ. In our Christian society of North America we are aware of Christ, and when we speak about Christ, others recognize him.

Recently I came across one of the most challenging passages about Jesus in the Gospel of John 14:7–14. Here Jesus tells us: "…the one who believes in me will also do the works that I do and, in fact, will do greater works than these." Wow! Jesus has just told us that if we believe in him, we will do greater works than he did. Is that possible? How can we surpass the miracles of Christ?

As I puzzled over this mind-boggling passage I remembered a discussion I had with a retired spiritualist, Father Reilly. He told me that envied me. He said that in my salvation story I had so much to present to God. My marriage and my children were such a great accomplishment. As a celibate, a priest, he said he had no such legacy, no such assurance of great works. I could not really agree with him. I pointed out to him that in a spiritual sense he was a "father" of many, and surely his works surpassed mine. But the encounter did make me realize again the significance of my life and the role I am to play in the kingdom of God.

And now I come across the words of Jesus telling us that our works will surpass his. Again, after reflection, there is a lesson to consider. Today it is possible to speak to many about Christ. We are at a different starting point than Jesus was. Look at Billy Graham as an extreme example. How many does he reach in a single telecast? Millions! He can do more to spread the kingdom than someone two thousand years ago, when Christianity was struggling and persecuted. You and I have all the advantages when it comes to spreading the Gospel. Today we send messages in cyberspace and have the technology to reach millions. We also have Jesus in heaven to assist us. After his ascension to the Father, Jesus promised to be with us in power and strength. Nothing is impossible to us: "I will do whatever you ask in my name, so that the Father may be glorified in the Son. If in my name you ask me for anything, I will do it" (John 14: 13–14). You and I can work in the Kingdom of God in ways Moses never dreamed of. In the *name* of Jesus, anything is possible!

We have a great reverence for the name of Jesus in our liturgies. We begin our celebrations in His name. We end our special prayers at funerals and weddings and other occasions "…through Jesus Christ, your son, who lives and reigns forever and ever." The name of Jesus is a powerful force in exorcism, faith healing, and in other intercessions to our Father: "We ask this in the name of Jesus." Before his crucifixion Jesus told his followers: "If in my name you ask me for anything, I will do it" (John 14:14).

Many of the saints often prayed by reverently repeating the holy name *Jesus*. Saint Ignatius of Loyola named his order of priests the Jesuits. Saint Francis de Sales frequently repeated the holy name and believed this would guarantee our dying a holy and happy death. Many of the saints spent their last days on earth frequently repeating "Jesus, Jesus." An aunt of mine, a saintly woman, was a member of the Order of St. Elizabeth stationed in Humbolt, Saskatchewan. As she was dying an agonizing death from cancer, she called on Jesus by name: "Come, Jesus, and get Sister Zita Rolheiser."

Repeating the name of Jesus in prayer or song can bring us a peace the world cannot give. The chanting of Jesus' name in song such as the Taize hymns, named after the part of France where this style originated, can be soul animating. If repeating the Lord's name is an effective way of helping us enter into those great moments of life, like marriage or death, perhaps we can get some badly needed help in facing the challenges of everyday life by simply repeating the holy name. This is a most powerful way the saints used to be more in touch with God.

BLESSINGS

> A double blessing is a double grace;
> Occasion smiles upon a second leave...
> There, my blessing with thee!

Shakespeare knew that blessing others was a common idea as Polonius blesses Laertes on his way to France in *Hamlet*. Blessings are common among us. Sneeze, and chances are you will receive a "Bless you!" or "Gesundheit!" which is a wish for good health. There is a heritage of blessings we may bestow on others as occasion makes them appropriate.

There is a great Irish blessing many are familiar with, often given when parting:

> May the road rise to meet you,
> May the wind be always at your back
> May the sun shine upon your face
> The rain fall soft upon your fields
> And, until we meet again,
> May God hold you in the palm of his hand.

On the lighter side, one Irish blessing that is perhaps not as familiar says:

> May those that love us, love us,
> And those that hate us, hate us,

May God turn their hearts.
And if He doesn't turn their hearts,
May He turn their ankles
So we will know them by their limping.

I like the terseness of another blessing attributed to the Irish: "May you be in heaven half an hour / Before the Devil knows you're dead."

Every baptized person is called to be a "blessing" and to bless. Laypeople may provide certain blessings, such as at a meal, but there are blessings pertaining to ecclesial and sacramental life that are reserved for the ordained ministry.

A Jewish blessing expressed in the word "barukh" does not mean bestowing a blessing in the normal sense, but it is an expression of wonder at how blessed the creator is. Thus, the creature does not bless the creator, but acknowledges a thankfulness.

One blessing my wife and I were fortunate enough to learn during our lay ministry training is a blessing we used to impart on our infant children before they fell asleep at night. A tremendous experience was when our children, as they were old enough, asked to bless us in turn, using the same prayer. I share it because it can be adapted for use with adults on occasions like when you bless someone who is ill. The blessing goes as follows: "May the Holy Spirit encircle you (make a circular motion over the head) with his love and joy and peace and give you a restful night. I sign you with the sign of the cross (anoint the forehead) and claim you for one of Jesus' own. (Holding your hand on recipient's head) May you have a good sleep and awake refreshed, ready to be a good child/servant of the Lord."

Blessings should be a natural and normal part of our lives as Christians. Recently at the funeral prayers of a friend I "signed" a "God bless you" as I paid a final respect. When you visit a sick person, especially in hospital, give him or her a blessing before you leave. One of the joys I have experienced is when one I bless returns the blessing. I now sometimes ask for a blessing before I leave a patient or a loved one.

The blessings we impart to others usually come back to us. They are a tremendous reminder of who we are, where we come from, and where we are going. May your life be blessed as you impart blessings on others: "A double blessing is a double grace."

I would like to conclude this chapter with a reflection on the importance of prayer in our hometown or community, and how we can make this prayer grow to include the wider world and its needs. Today, more than ever, the world is a village. Wouldn't it be great if everyone had the same spirit of loyalty to our planet and everyone on it that you find in small towns around the world?

People have fierce loyalties to their communities, their schools, their sports teams. We've all heard the slogan "be true to your school!" What if we enlarged that concept a little to include your *town*, your *country*, and your *planet*. Being loyal to your school demands commitment. Taken seriously, it means you work to make it a better place; you are concerned about spirit. Ultimately, it takes a commitment of soul. I often wonder who is responsible to pray for the teachers and students in a school. Do the parents do that? As a teacher I've become a little more serious about this facet of school spirit. It's a daily need.

Who prays for the town/city? And who is responsible for community spirit? Is it the job of town council? When you are tempted to say "they haven't got a prayer," be careful. Whose fault is that? If you are a regular churchgoer you realize that prayers are occasionally said for town, for government, for the world. But there is a real everyday need.

Then we come to the planet, the environment, and ultimately, the Kosovos and Afghanistans of the world. Much prayer is needed to soften the hearts of those who cause such unnatural structures. Jesus said, "Ask the Father for anything in my name and he will give it to you." One of the most powerful prayers I've come across, that is big enough for world problems, I picked up from the Good Friday liturgy. It is a prayer we need to repeat at those times when we see the starving and freezing refugees, those times when we want to storm heaven to change the injustices of the world: "For the sake of your Son, have mercy, Lord." Where there is suffering in the world, Christ is there:

"For the sake of your Son, have mercy, Lord." Ask our Father who loved this world so much he allowed the suffering and death of his own Son: "For the sake of your Son, have mercy, Lord."

Prayer is a mystery. How God answers our prayers we do not often understand. We only know that God can use our prayers, our lives and our will to solve the biggest problems of this world. Alfred Lord Tennyson said, "More things are wrought by prayer than this world dreams of." Part of the mystery of prayer is learning to listen to God.

CHAPTER NINE

Forgiveness

Stabbed repeatedly, eleven-year-old Maria Goretti lies dying. She says about the man who stabbed her and tried to rape her: "For the love of Jesus I forgive him...and I want him to be with me in paradise." Saint Maria Goretti dies shortly after. She forgave Alexander, a neighbor's son, even before he repented of his crime. Twenty-seven years later, Alexander is released from prison. A changed man, he seeks Maria's mother and asks her forgiveness. At first, it is too much to ask! It is her daughter's killer, and he is asking her to forgive him. She invites him in and they go to midnight Mass together, receiving Holy Communion together. She forgives him. Her explanation: "I looked to the Lord who forgave his murderers on the cross, and I tried to follow his example. As Jesus hung on the cross dying, he asked the Father to forgive us. Why is it sometimes so hard for us to forgive each other?"

> Slowly the man's head is placed on the guillotine. The slotted wooden bars are fastened securely over his neck, ready for the sharp blade. The executioner's hand reaches for the release. But just then, behind the executioner, a voice of authority is heard: "I desire mercy, and not sacrifice." The executioner turns with a start and recognizes Jesus. He looks at the condemned man. It's his next door neighbor! Finally—and here is the greatest surprise—the executioner removes his hood. He is...you! (from *The Word Among Us,* July 19, 2002).

How often we criticize and condemn the people around us. How often we make hasty judgments on our neighbor and even on family members. "Forgive us...as we forgive those who trespass against us." Forgiveness is Good News. Our heavenly Father wants to forgive us.

The story is told of a nun in the Middle Ages who was having visions of God. The bishop wanted proof, so he asked the nun to ask God what the bishop's great sin had been before he entered the priesthood. Next time the nun came to see him, he asked her if she had asked the Lord. She said, "Yes." Anxiously the bishop asked, "What did he say it was?" The nun said, "He said, 'I forgot'."

When I first started working on this chapter on repentance, I realized I had called the chapter "Forgiveness" and not "Repentance." I suddenly realized that "forgiveness" is a word that brings warm feeling to the heart. "Repentance" has a bad reputation, but it is ill deserved. Perhaps we have heard zealous evangelists shouting: "Repent! Repent!" Actually repentance is a rewarding action, a treasure. How did the prodigal son (Luke 15:11–32) feel when he came back into his father's arms? Much better than when he was swilling hogs in a foreign land.

God our Father has always loved us. He does not shake his head in disgust over our weaknesses. He wants to strengthen the weak and raise up the fallen. He does not demand blood for our sins: "I desire mercy and not sacrifice" (Matthew 12:7). Forgiveness comes from love, and God is love. If we love God, we will keep his commandments. And that should be good news for our neighbor.

I'm sure you have heard the prophets of gloom and doom on a gorgeous, sunny day saying: "We will pay for it!" I usually respond with something like, "We've paid for it already, last winter." The *great* news is that we are bought and paid for: "...as one man's trespass led to condemnation for all, so one man's [Christ's] act of righteousness leads to justification and life for all" (Romans 5:18). I don't want to be too hard on Adam, our first parent, for I know that, given the chance, I would have messed up in like fashion. I've proved that many times.

The *great* hope that you and I cling to is that, "While we were yet sinners Christ died for us" (Romans 5:8). In the hierarchy of virtues, forgiveness is near the top, though love comes first. Maria Goretti's forgiveness is an example. Christ gave us another: Jesus hangs from the cross in agony. Tortured and abused for hours, treated with hatred and contempt, abandoned by his closest friends, physically and emotionally drained, what does Jesus do? He forgives his tormentors: "Father, forgive them; for they do not know what they are doing" (Luke 23:34).

That is the great news. You and I, even though we can never hope to merit it, are redeemed by the love of a forgiving Christ. Karl Rahner in *Prayers for a Lifetime* says, "Most of the time when we sin, we do know what we are doing, but we don't know how much God loves us—hence we are still innocent through ignorance." Christ's love redeems us and fills us with hope. Gloom, despair and agony fade away.

DARK NIGHT OF THE SOUL

Since the coming of Christ and even before that light has been a symbol of God. The light in Peter's prison reveals the angel of deliverance (Acts 12:7); in his conversion Saint Paul recognizes God's presence in a blinding light; the Transfiguration shows God's presence as light (Matthew 17:5); and the light of heaven shines on the shepherds at the birth of Christ. In our liturgies the light of the candle signifies the light of Christ. Our world is very familiar with the symbolism of light. How is it then that we struggle so frequently in a darkness of soul?

Our greatest saints like Mother Teresa struggle with feelings of abandonment. Sometimes she "...felt rejected by God, helpless and tempted to abandon her work" ("Mother Teresa Felt Rejected by God," *Leader Post Regina*, Saturday, September 15, 2001). The article goes on to describe in her own words how Mother Teresa sometimes felt "...the terrible pain of loss, of God not wanting me, of God not being God, of God not really existing." But Mother Teresa clung to Jesus in faith. She constantly told God how much she longed for him. She simply accepted the dark moments as part of the darkness and pain Christ experienced on earth. "I simply offer myself to Jesus," she said.

The greatest mystics have struggled with what John of the Cross called "the dark night of the soul." Martin Luther felt he was fighting Satan's attacks. Dietrich Bonhoeffer wrote poems of doubt and abandonment by God, even as he conducted worship services and ministered in the Nazi concentration camp. Small wonder you and I at times struggle with spiritual darkness that tests our faith. Does God really exist? Why is he not answering my prayers? Is it because I am an unworthy sinner? In our moments of darkness we are in good company. When we have doubts and fears, God is near. Saint Paul says, "Jesus came into the world to save sinners—of whom I am the foremost" (and I thought I was). Paul goes on "...I received mercy, so that in me, as the foremost, Jesus Christ might display the utmost patience, making me an example to those who would come to believe in him for eternal life" (1 Timothy 1:15–17).

Our darkness of mind seems almost a permanent condition when we consider the prevalence of war, violence and hatred in the history of mankind. North versus South, the Hill people versus the Valley people, husband versus wife, the list goes on. There is discord and dismay in many communities, families and social organizations. It seems to be a human condition. But there is a better way to live.

In the movie *War of the Roses* we see how absurd conflict can get when the couple, played by Michael Douglas and Kathleen Turner, literally try to kill each other. By that time there is little hope for their marriage, though they still appear to be in love. There is nothing civil about a civil war. And marital arguments tend to be uncivil if we let them. In marriage conflict we need to weigh the sake of the relationship. Do we want to dissolve this marriage over this disagreement? Do we have the will to hang in there and see the big picture? Is the marriage worth more than this one disagreement? Then there is the family to consider—children and even the larger community that is hurt by the discord.

This principle of compromise applies to community conflict as well. Collectively we need to see the big picture and decide how important our egos are. So many times couples break up because they can't see the big picture. Ironically, they may still be in love with each other, but they do not have the grace to compromise. Give a little here to save the lot! In the community it is hoped cooler heads can prevail, but I have seen enough of human nature to wonder if this is so.

In his poem "Worms and the Wind" Carl Sandburg says:

> Zigzag worms hate circle worms,
> Curve worms never trust square worms.
> ...
> When worms go to war they dig in, come out and fight, dig in
> again, come out and fight again, dig in again, and so on.
> Worms underground never hear the wind overground and
> sometimes they ask,
> "What is this wind we hear of?"

Jesus gives us a better way. The Bible often compares our relationship to God to a marriage (see Hosea). We may be unfaithful, but He is forever faithful. As we become more like God's son, we will be peacemakers in our marriages and in our communities. Our world at large is still struggling in darkness of mind, "digging in, coming out to fight, digging in again..." Mankind will not be judged by the wars we have waged, but by the way we have received the love Christ has "waged." He literally stormed the closed gates of heaven with his prayerful love as he was dying: "Father, forgive them..."

I once wrote an article entitled "Fire and Flintstone." No, it was not a typo, I insisted. I meant to say flintstone because you can get a spark from flint. Brimstone is sulfur and it burns. I am reminded of the fire and brimstone sermons I heard as a child. These attempted to scare the "hell" out of me, with some success. I would rather have had a spark engendered in me that would have led me in a constructive spiritual direction earlier in life.

A friend of mine recently asked me to write about judgment and hell, hoping I would address the idea of universal salvation, that some believe God will save all. I gathered she felt this concept was in error.

My immediate answer was that we can refuse salvation, as free creatures, but I was guarded about the rest of the question. But the conversation set me thinking: "Love and peace of God, or the fire of hell?"

As a child I developed a scrupulous conscience. For a time I had nightmares and believed I was going to hell. Nothing could save me. Somehow the stories told to me by the good nuns and the missionary preachers about a God who was absolute in punishing a sinful mistake you make, even if only once, caused me great unrest. I'd much rather have heard of a loving God who encourages you to grow away from sin and into his love.

Imagine for a moment the mind of Christ on the night before his death as he is reflecting on the salvation of the world. Is he considering that only a select few will be saved? Is he going to die tomorrow in a futile attempt to save the majority, or is his love all-embracing and magnanimous? Is his act of love good news to the sinner or is it condemnation? I think we can get some direction about this mystery by the words and actions of Jesus Christ on the day of his death.

In agony Jesus cries out about those who are persecuting, torturing and killing him: "Father, forgive them. They know not what they are doing." In generosity Jesus turns to the thief at his side and says, "Today you will be with me in paradise." But like you and me, and all those who face the darkness of pain, suffering and death, Jesus is very human and cries out, "My God, My God, why have you forsaken me?"

Fire and flint! Jesus came to start a fire, the fire of his Spirit of love: "I came to bring fire to the earth and how I wish it were already kindled!" (Luke 12:19). He came to strike a spark in us so we can explode into light and be the light to a world in darkness. He came to push back the gates of hell and the threat of God. He came to reveal the heart of love in the Father. "Peace I leave with you. My peace I give you." He did not come to bring nightmares to children, but to bring us the joy of hope. He wants us to have a Father, someone we can call "Abba" or "Daddy."

I was raised with the Latin rites and rituals and the Requiem Mass for funerals. The "Day of Wrath" which described the day of judgment made me tremble with fear. Fortunately my education about sin and judgment did not end there. Through the loving trust of my parents, a church transformed by Vatican II, and my growing understanding of God's love, I eventually learned to trust God and to expect a warm heart at the end of my pilgrim journey.

Nothing is hidden from God! He sees all the wrongs we do! But he also sees all the good actions. In Hebrews 6:10 Saint Paul says, "For God is not unjust; he will not overlook your work and the love that you showed for his sake in serving the saints, as you still do." And who are the saints? The people of God in general, everyone set apart for the Lord through faith and baptism; our father and mother, our brothers and sisters are saints. Our children are saints. The people we sit next to in church are the saints, God's chosen ones.

One example from Scripture will help us understand the heart of Jesus, the heart of God. Jesus sought the house of sinners when he called Levi and went to eat at his place. I enjoy Luke's version (5:27–32) where Levi, in response to the call by Jesus to follow him, holds a big reception where tax collectors and others are gathered with Levi and Jesus. The Scribes and Pharisees complain, "Why do you eat and drink with tax collectors and sinners?" And Jesus replies, "Those who are well have no need of a physician, but those who are sick. I have come to call not the righteous but sinners to repentance." Jesus is calling us and seeking us out. And he is calling us to the service of the saints, those around us that he has called. There is some consolation in the old adage, "You are known by the company you keep." We can cast away our fear of judgment; nothing should inhibit us from caring for the saints. Christ has put away sin once and for all by sacrificing himself. After that atonement, our part is easy. Jesus is our big brother, drawing all people together. In loving the poor and those around us, others will come to know the same freedom, and God's kingdom will grow.

Are we fully convinced that Jesus loves us and that we are part of this community of saints I have been describing? Many are not. A soldier asked an abbot if God would show him mercy. The old monk asked the soldier: "Tell me, beloved, if your cloak were torn would you throw it away?" He said: "Nay, I would patch it and wear it." The abbot replied: "If you would spare a garment, shall not God have mercy on God's own image?"

Too often we feel down about our spiritual selves. We seek gloom to match our moods, and often we gravitate toward "sad news." Listen to any newscast; check any newspaper. As Christians we would do better to give a positive spin to our lives and to seek the actions that make us Christians. Albert Einstein said: "I don't know what destiny all of you are called to, but the only ones of you who will be really happy are those who realize you are called to serve."

Over and over again in the Bible Jesus says, "Peace be with you" and "Repent and believe the Good News." Why should we ever feel gloomy and hopeless? Three hundred and sixty-five times in the Bible God tells us, "Be not afraid." That is enough to cover every day of the year. It is also a strong hint that we need to remind ourselves frequently of the hope that is central to our lives. We are the Resurrection People. The Risen Christ is among us and in us. "How beautiful upon the mountains are the feet of the messenger...who announces peace" (Isaiah 52:7). God's loving arms are reaching out to a world crying out in a suicide of despair. Hope and joy are not reserved for wise monks and mystics. We must believe that there is a God who longs to fill our spiritual hungers, in spite of our sins.

Our sins are the biggest obstacle to our accepting God's plan for our salvation. We need to leave the gloom of our sins behind and to focus on the good news of our salvation. Many live with a callous disregard for the spiritual, the sacred. Shakespeare's Hamlet said,

> ...What is a man,
> If his chief good and market of his time
> Be but to sleep and feed? a beast, no more.
> Sure He that made us with such large discourse,
> Looking before and after, gave us not
> That capability and godlike reason
> To fust in us unus'd (*Hamlet* IV, iv, 33–39).

God created us with a capability to understand and seek the truth. And God cares about us, whether we live or die, in a spiritual sense. God has given you and me a heart of flesh. We care about our neighbors. We do not live in isolation but crave society. "No man is an island; every man is a piece of the continent, a part of the main" (John Donne). In Donne's reflection he goes on to talk about our interconnectedness. But in these pages I want to talk more about the good news that God cares about us.

In Ezekiel 36:23–28 God reveals to us his plan for the nations. He will reveal himself to the nations and gather us from all countries: "I will sprinkle clean water upon you, and you shall be clean...I will remove from your body the heart of stone and...give you a heart of flesh. I will put my spirit within you...you shall be my people, and I will be your God." Wow! How better to move from guilt and sadness (our normal preoccupation) to healing and action?

Talk about a heart transplant! God takes our hearts of stone and makes it possible for us to soften our hearts. He makes it possible for us to forgive others, to love. He makes it possible for us to turn from sin and move with a free and open heart. We have a new heart and a new lease on life. In the fullness of time God sent his prophets, and in the fullness of time he sent his own son Jesus to reveal the Truth to us. As a creature, I need to give thanks daily for the gifts of the creator. "Thank you God."

JOY
In moving this chapter from the many thoughts related to darkness, gloom and agony, though I tried to dispel the gloom as we went, I want to lead the reader to reflect briefly on our job in the Kingdom of God. How do we prepare and stay fit for the quest? A simple answer is that we need to know Jesus better. And the best source to tap is to read Scripture daily. God talks to us through his prophets and Jesus talks to us through the Gospel writings. Daily reading and reflection on the Word of God will help us to get to know Jesus and the nature of God. And God is Love and forgiveness. The stories of the Bible tell us of many terrible sinners who became great saints.

A couple of examples come to mind. In Genesis we read about Joseph who was sold by his brothers and ended up in Egypt. His brothers eventually feel remorse for their action and a certain amount of fear because Joseph has now become a powerful lord in charge of the storehouses of Egypt. As Joseph reveals his identity to Reuben and his other brothers, they are afraid (Genesis 45), but he says, "God sent me before you to preserve life." Sometimes God uses our mistakes to bring about a good purpose. God has plans to use even his unworthy servants like you and me. Just as he used Moses, who at one low point in his life had killed an Egyptian, hid him in the sand, and was hiding from the Pharaoh (Exodus 11:22); so God also used David, who committed adultery and arranged the death of an innocent man. Then there was Saint Peter who denied Jesus three times loudly and clearly. God used all of these sinners to show us the way back to the Kingdom. Their examples of repentance can be an inspiration.

The point is that maybe, with the help of the Holy Spirit, God can work wonders through us. We dare to hope that the Lord can use us. So far I've been able to avoid inflicting murderous adultery and violent persecutions on others. Did I mention Saint Paul and his zeal to arrest Christians? He probably got an assist in the death of Saint Stephen. Being a Christian today should be easier. It is often very hard to love the person sitting next to us at the table. But it should be easy, especially if the day is very hot: "...whoever gives even a cup of cold water to one of these little ones in the name of a disciple—truly I tell you, none of these will lose their reward" (Matthew 10:42).

Speaking of Saint Paul, I recently I had a dream. I saw a focal point of light trying to break through to my vision. As I gazed, it seemed to be about to emanate towards me, a light that could expand and grow. The following morning I read the Mass readings for the day and was surprised to see the story of Saint Paul's conversion on the road to Damascus. The light of Christ knocked Paul off his "high horse," so to speak, and blinded him (Acts 22:3–16). The voice said to Paul, "I am Jesus of Nazareth whom you are persecuting." And Jesus further instructed him, "The God of our ancestors has chosen you to know his will, to see the Righteous One and to hear his own voice. Get up, be baptized and have your sins washed away, calling on his name."

The point is that Jesus calls us while we are yet sinners. Often we are paralyzed from right action because we think that we are unworthy sinners. If we compare ourselves to Saint Paul in his unholy zeal to harm Christians, we know that the Lord can work through us just as easily. The leap of faith to trust in God is not then so great. If you have been focused on the negative aspects of your life and have allowed them to hinder your Christian action, open up your eyes and heart. We are redeemed, cleansed by the blood of Christ, and filled by the Holy Spirit; and we are required to become active in working for the Kingdom. Watch today for the opportunity to share Christ's love with someone you meet in the ordinary circumstances of life.

The small light I saw in my dream may have been a reminder to me to have the courage to attempt that task that is going to require hard work and faith. I know what it is now, and I know that it is possible if the Spirit is in me and if I can get off my "high horse" and focus on the simple task of faith that lies before me. How do I do this?

How do you and I achieve what we scarcely dare to dream? Let me answer with a little anecdote. I remember a fellow, actually he was a Director of Education, who wanted to be a *one* when asked to rate his administrative set-up from one to ten. His confusion was that he thought *one* was like "number one." Enough years have passed that I can now use this example which was rather humorous at the time (his critics agreed with his rating). I guess he was not a Bo Derek fan.

In the story of the ten lepers (Luke 17:11–19) only *one* came back to thank Jesus for the cure. How can you and I be that *one* out of ten? When was the last time you thanked God for your breath, your health, and your blessings? It is so easy to continue on our way when things are going well.

I picked up some inspiration recently when I spoke with my son who works in computer chip design. His job is challenging and complex to the nth degree. The process he is involved with includes teams working in different cities and each developing aspects of this multi-faceted high-speed interface chip. At later stages of development component parts of the program are assembled and their functions tested. If there are any problems, it's troubleshooting time and my son works at solutions. The process is very demanding. After speaking with him, I realized that my writing career had picked up some much-needed inspiration. The process of planning a chapter of a book and organizing ideas into understandable and logical patterns seemed infinitely less complex than the literally millions of letters, numbers and symbols that make up a computer interface chip, the size of a quarter.

Here's what I mean: "PMC-Sierra [his company] is a leading provider of high speed broadband communications and storage semi-conductors and MIPS-based processors for Service Provider, Enterprise, Storage, and wireless networking equipment." In the past year PMCS has put some 25 devices on the market. Here is their most recent: "PMC-Sierra, Inc. introduced the PM3393 S/UNI 1x10GE-XP, a highly integrated, low power, all-purpose Ethernet solution for use in enterprise, storage, and metro applications."

Suddenly I was happy to be working on the job I believe the Lord is calling me to do. We each have certain talents and we need to use these talents for the good of all. If we want to shine like Olympic stars, perhaps we need to apply ourselves to the daily practice and routines as an Olympic star does. The discipline of proper diet, exercise (working) and rest routines become significant. What should make it much easier for us as Christians is that we are accepting this calling as disciples with the knowledge of God's supporting Grace and Providence. Jesus in our lives makes it possible. We also have the deep assurance of God's love.

I once tried to intrigue the readers of my spiritual column with an article entitled "Butterfly 10." It began with this little anecdote: An Englishman, an Italian, a Frenchman and a German were discussing the poetic nature of their languages. The Englishman said, "Take the word 'butterfly.' It is so exact, so accurate, so descriptive." The Italian said, "Our word is 'mariposa,' 'mariposa.' It is so apt, almost musical." The Frenchman said, "We have the best word for butterfly, 'papillon'!

It is musical and descriptive." The German spoke up, "Und vat ist wrong mit 'schmetterling'?"

A discussion with a reader of my previous column "Are You a Ten?" had inspired me to reflect on the delicate and priceless beauty of an emerging butterfly (it also gave me an excuse to share the joke). Let me explain: to some readers of that article I might have seemed a little smug and comfortable in my role as a spiritual writer. It sounds like a worthwhile, if not glamorous job. That was not the viewpoint I was trying to convey, but it set me thinking. Each one of us is so special; our names are carved in the palm of God's hand (Isaiah 49:15–16).

No matter what our daily work is, we are surrounded by signs and wonders in our lives. We carry a dignity as God's creatures—through baptism we are brothers and sisters of Christ, members of the same family. He who made the butterfly also made us. If we don't see miraculous signs and wonders in our simple existence, it is perhaps because we don't need them to have a strong faith; or maybe, and this is more likely, we are in tune with the daily miracles and gifts from the creator—the sunset, fresh air, lungs to breathe, the taste of cold water, the warmth of a hug.

There is a certain security in love. I know what it is to look on my children from the precious age of infancy, to watch them grow and blossom into priceless young men and women. I've watched them leave the cocoon of youth and emerge into butterflies. Their use of God's gifts, their developing skills and careers are so precious to witness. Do you think our heavenly Father feels less pride in each of us as we mature and go to work in the vineyard of the world? We are loved!

Priceless is the word! "God so loved the world that he gave his only Son, so that everyone who believes in him may not perish but may have eternal life" (John 3:16). Picture the heart of our heavenly Father—the pride and joy in his son as Jesus grew up to manhood. Picture our Father watching Jesus match wits with the rabbis in the temple. On occasion God our Father couldn't hold back his pride. At the transfiguration the heavens opened and a voice boomed, "This is my Son, the Beloved...listen to him!" (Matthew 17:5). Picture also the anguish in watching his son sacrifice himself on the cross, for us. How can we doubt our importance? When it comes to describing the significance of each one of us to God, we are a ten; we are a butterfly and a ten.

Another analogy that comes close to describing the spiritual reality that is Jesus in our lives is the metaphor of rock. Peter was chosen as the rock of the church. In the same way you and I are chosen by God to be a part of this church, the Body of Christ on earth. In this sense we are rocks, building blocks of the church. Sometimes, when we are most filled with zealous joy, we may even be accused of being "stoned."

How about you and me today? Are we experiencing the joy and peace of Jesus in our lives right now? How do we connect to the Rock of Ages, to give us a solid faith to sustain us through life's trials? The Good News is that Jesus is always inviting us first. Despite our sins God approaches us in subtle, tender ways, if we learn to listen. In John 4:5–42 we find an excellent example of this in the story of the Samaritan woman at the well. Jesus surprised her by talking to her, since she was both a Samaritan and a woman. He tells her her sins, that the man she is with is not her husband. She knew that when the Messiah comes, "he will proclaim all things to us." In her joy at finding the Lord she leaves her water jar at the well and runs to tell everyone about Jesus.

It takes just a little effort to turn our lives toward Jesus. Even though sin is still in our lives, we can start to realize the tremendous love God has for us and turn toward the Lord. That's all it takes. Once our hearts are open to the Lord, he will lead us through His Spirit. Like the woman at the well, we can leave our sins behind and run with joy to tell everyone about God's love. We know what it is like when we are wronged by someone we really love. Imagine a loving husband and father devoted to his wife and family. Imagine what he would feel if his wife accused him of being unfaithful and took the children and abandoned him. How does God feel when we (sometimes with our whole family) abandon him who is still faithful and loves us?

Saint Augustine once said, "Could anyone refuse to love our God, so abounding in mercy, so just in his ways? Could anyone deny love of him who first loved us despite all our injustice and all our pride?" Christ's love redeems our innocence and gives us hope. All we have to do is turn our steps toward him.

In the past year I have discovered an adequate comparison to describe the joyous impact of the Good News on us as messengers of Jesus. Imagine the feet of an amateur climber the morning after he climbs his first big mountain. I know from the experience of family members who have felt this particular pain. Simply walking downstairs was too painful, so they turned and went down the staircase backwards. The question is what could possibly be so great and awe-inspiring that they would feel happiness in their steps that morning? It is the Good News of Jesus.

"How beautiful upon on the mountain are the feet of the messenger...who brings good news" (Isaiah 52:7). One of my objectives in *Pause for Reflection* is to lift us up to God's loving arms reaching out to a world crying out in despair. Elie Wiesel says his two favorite words are "And yet." They are applicable to every situation, happy or bleak. The sun is rising? Any yet it will set. A night of anguish? And yet, it too will pass. The important thing is to shun resignation, to refuse to wallow in sterile fatalism. Happiness is in the one who brings good news. Even the feet that climb on the mountain are happy with Good News.

The story is told of Saint Francis of Assisi who one day met an acquaintance who looked troubled and asked him: "Brother, how are things with you?" The man started raving, "Thanks to my master— may God curse him!—I have had nothing but misfortune. He has taken away all I possess."

Francis, filled with pity, said, "Brother, pardon your master for the love of God, and free your own soul; it's possible that he will restore to you whatever he has taken away. Otherwise, you have lost your goods and will lose your soul as well." But the man persisted, "I can't fully forgive him unless he returns what he has taken from me."

Francis insisted, "Look, I will give you this cloak; I beg you to forgive your master for the love of the Lord God." The man's heart was melted by this kindness and he forgave his master. Immediately he was filled with joy.

Like Saint Francis, our role is to serve others as Christ would. By spreading the joy and freedom that we are heirs to as followers of Christ, we become the arms of Christ reaching out to a world which desperately needs peace and joy. The warmth of that embrace can bring joy and peace, no matter how desperate the situation of our lives.

It is no secret that the joy of Christ's message is thriving best in developing countries, among the poorest of the poor. To them God's words in Isaiah 55 are easier to understand, though they bring as much consolation to everyone of faith:

> Ho, everyone who thirsts,
>   come to the waters;
> And you that have no money,
>   come, buy and eat!
> Come, buy wine and milk
>   without money and without price
> Why do you spend your money for that which is not
>   bread,
>   and your labor for that which does not satisfy?
> Listen carefully to me, and eat what is good,
>   and delight yourselves in rich food.
> Incline your ear, and come to me;
>   listen, so that you may live.

True peace will come to those who, like Saint Francis of Assisi, become a channel of Christ's peace. Where there is hatred, they sow love; where there is injury, they bring forgiveness; where there is doubt and fear, they bring faith; where there is sadness, they bring joy; where there is despair, they bring hope; and where there is darkness, they bring light.

REPENTANCE

We have all seen the TV talk show's physical makeovers. Probably too many times. But have we ever thought of what an amazing change a spiritual makeover can effect? The "before" picture and the "after" picture? Is it the same human being?

The other day I was giving my computer system a makeover, that is, purging it of viruses, and I was led to reflect briefly on its worth. Earlier in the day, as I was struggling to download an Internet program and the computer froze on me, after a half-hour struggle, I felt that maybe this was a piece of junk, a mathematical box that didn't function smoothly. Later, as the anti-virus program raced through twenty-seven thousand files, I started to change my thinking. A virus was located and purged. Thousands of files were scanned and pronounced "clean." Then I started thinking of a spiritual analogy.

You and I have billions of neurons that make up our ability to think. Additionally, we have a physical life that provides electrical stimuli to fire the synapses between these neurons, causing them to form thought patterns, somehow linking us to our eternal instincts. Somehow we are connected to a God who gives us a sense of right and wrong, a sense of worth and well-being, and who gives us many other "files" that contain our spiritual and moral training and development.

How do we feel when we have sinned and infected our spiritual life and well-being? We feel like a useless lump of clay. Our greater purpose has been diminished, and we wonder about our overall worth. Sometimes we "scan" these "down" feelings and find a virus that has been infecting us spiritually. How free and clear, how wonderful we feel when, with the help of the Holy Spirit and God's forgiveness, we can scratch out that infection. Suddenly the billions of neurons fire happily. Our thoughts are racing freely again, and we feel like a million clean and useful files. The "after" picture of our spiritual makeover is truly amazing. We hardly recognize what we once were. That is the gift of forgiveness.

How do we achieve repentance for our sins and a contrite heart? Let me illustrate. Suppose a big limousine pulled up at your door and Ed McMahon delivered the Publisher's Clearing House $10,000,000?

A much greater fortune is ours and we have only to realize it to col-
lect. In Hebrews 10 the Lord says, "I will remember their sins and
their lawless deeds no more." Christ "sat down at the right hand of
God" and made his enemies a footstool.

A difficult concept for us to understand is that before we were
born, Christ had died for our sins and the sins of all mankind. It is
not something we earned or something that we deserved. But it is
something we can grow to accept. Let us suppose that before you were
born your father sacrificed his life so that you could be free. He knew
that only by dying could he win the political freedom that would create the kind of society that you could safely grow up in. This is not
unlike the sacrifice some of our relatives made during the world wars.
Now what kind of gratitude and love would you feel when you
matured enough to recognize your father's great sacrifice? How close
would you feel to him? How readily would you accept and safeguard
that precious freedom?

One of the most difficult concepts we struggle with as Christians
is *repentance*. Since Adam's sin, our first fall from grace, our pride has
not diminished. We are still afraid to admit the nakedness of our sins,
metaphorically speaking. Even the great cry of repentance from TV
evangelists does not touch all. The story is told of a congregation whose
pastor was away on a holiday. In an effort to surprise him they decided
to paint the rectory and church. They were running short of paint as
they neared the end of the job, so they added some thinner to enable
them to finish. Upon his return the pastor inspected their efforts.
Finally he said, "Repaint, you thinners!" All kidding aside, "repent
and be saved" does not ring a true note to many. Pride may not be the
only problem here. In fact, sometimes it is our intelligence that gets in
the way. But it is our intelligence that can help us in the end.

One thing that can help us toward true repentance is first of all to
become aware of what it means. Repentance means a change of mind
or heart, that is, a change of intention, disposition, attitude; it means
regret, conversion and sorrow for sin. Turning to the Lord should be
easy. Think of how Luke announces the joy of salvation to the world
in the famous Christmas narrative when the angel says: "I am bring-

ing you good news of great joy for all the people: to you is born this day...a savior who is the Messiah, the Lord." Yes! We can buy that: "God and sinner reconciled," "Joy to the World," "Faith of our Fathers."

Repentance is presented to us by Mark 1:15: "Repent, and believe in the good news." For too long "repentance" has had us focused on sin and punishment and not on the *turning to God's love.* Think of the Good News that Jesus came to announce. Salvation has been won for us. We cannot make amends for our sins through our own efforts. We merely have to become aware of God's love for his children. What is needed is a simple turning towards God's love and an acceptance of the Good News of salvation.

The best example of God's great love for us is the illustration Jesus uses in the Prodigal Son story (Luke 15:11–32). The Father is always turned towards us, watching and waiting for us to return. He carries no big stick (except for the fatted calf) and he is always waiting, watching for us. What keeps us from returning to his warm embrace? The exciting aspect to me is that we merely have to turn to the Lord as the prodigal son did, walking toward his father. For too long we have been turned from the Lord out of pride or fear of punishment. If we only knew of the Father's love and believed in his love, we would beat a path to our true home. Our sins and everything else would be as nothing! And what a joyous reunion there would be. Repentance is a change of heart, a returning. Because of our pride repentance for our sins is a tough pill for us to swallow! But how much easier it is to recognize Christ's sacrifice, and in so doing, turn toward that love that has won our priceless freedom.

Thinking about death and the final judgment is a traditional way to focus on repentance. When I was a child I used to say a prayer after Communion that included: "From this moment I accept whatsoever death Thou shalt send me, with its sorrows and afflictions [and a few other words I did not understand]...and in union with Christ I offer this up in reparation for my sins and the sins of others..."

What I am about to say may sound foolish in terms of the values of this world, but we should rejoice when we see that first sign of arthritis that comes with age. We should rejoice at that first bout with cancer. Recently, after jogging, I could feel a pain in my ankles and realized I was no longer a spry fifty-year-old. But to me the tingle in my ankles and the stiff muscles when I get up in the morning are a sign of the victory to come. I realize it is very easy to be cerebral in the absence of real pain, but it is still a matter of perspective. Eventually death will take us. We will lose the battle for good health and fitness. Cancer or Alzheimer's is not the end, but the beginning. Death is not the end but the beginning. Our moment of death will be the greatest moment of our existence. It will be the time to rejoice in Christ's victory over death.

How our audit stands at the moment of death is something we pre-occupy ourselves with. If we are not perfect at the moment of death, and chances are good we will not be, we will be ready for the final experience of God's mercy. Purgatory, as some Christian churches call it, is feared by many. The best explanation I have come across to describe the passage from imperfection to heavenly perfection involves a little parable.

The story is told of a promiscuous young man, given to drugs and alcohol abuse, careless of personal hygiene and appearance. One day this youth sees a beautiful woman. His attraction to her is over-whelming, but he realizes he is totally unworthy of her. He decides then and there that he will change his life around. In anticipation of her love, he cleans up his appearance, goes on a rehabilitation pro-gram for his chemical dependencies, gets a job and cleans up his life.

This parable explains what our state may be like when we meet the Lord after our life on earth is completed. The mere presence of the goodness of God will make us want to become perfect, to be worthy of that eternal union, that eternal love. We may not know exactly what the conditions or state of purgatory after death may be like, but we know some of the absolute principles involved. God's love for us is sure. Christ came to reveal that love of the Father to us. As we learn of God's love, we are attracted to a lifestyle that is less indulgent and more disciplined, more giving. We want to become worthy of so great a love. Nothing unclean will be in the presence of God who is pure love. Purgatory, the final purification, will not be a great surprise to us, especially if we have already begun the process on earth.

In the way of conclusion to this comparatively lengthy chapter I want to dwell briefly on our state of readiness or worthiness for the Kingdom. In the weekend sessions of my lay ministries training course I used to share a room with a lawyer who talked in his sleep. Shortly after drifting off he would say, "I'm ready!" This was a frequent occurrence in the restive start of his night's sleep. Eventually I drew a reflection from it.

When God called Samuel to be a prophet, Samuel's response was: "I'm ready Lord, use me." Samuel was lying in the sanctuary of Yahweh when he heard God call, "Samuel! Samuel!" After running to Eli and discerning that it must be God calling him, Samuel's response was "Speak, LORD, for your servant is listening" (1 Samuel 3:9).

Are we ready? In our day-to-day spiritual growth the one thing that holds us back is our sinfulness. "I'm not worthy!" is our stock response. We need to make that leap of faith that allows us to be "wounded healers." Though sinners ourselves, we can yet serve and heal others. Don't be afraid of piety and humility!

Saint Peter definitely was not worthy to be chosen head of the church, to be responsible for the whole future of Christianity; yet Christ chose him. It was only when Peter realized his utter nothingness after betraying Christ that he was "ready" to be remade in the image of Christ. It is only after we humbly bow to our nothingness and emptiness that we can say, "I'm ready, Lord; use me!"

I often remind me of Saint Peter. It's not a flattering comparison. Sometimes when I reflect on my behavior, the word "jackass" comes to mind. It's at times like that when I think of Saint Peter. "How could I have been so stupid? What am I using for brains? Will God forgive me?" Of course Jesus welcomes us back. All it took for Saint Peter was for Jesus to look at him. Peter did betray Jesus three times, loud and clear, before the cock crowed twice! And that was after swearing up and down that he would stand by Jesus and defend him no matter what!

As we go down life's path we are aware of sin and weakness. We set our sights farther down the trail and carry on. What made Saint

Peter a great saint is the repentance and the adjustments he made when he realized his betrayal of Christ.

Jesus looked at Saint Peter and loved him. He looks at us and loves us, too. He does not judge us by the mistakes we make on our journey, but by the eventual direction we choose. Like Saint Peter we need to be able to admit our mistakes and turn to God for forgiveness. Maybe it's pride, but the one thing that is really difficult for most of us to admit, honestly, is that we are sinners. That's the one thing Saint Peter owned up to freely.

So we read the signs in our day-to-day experience of God, and we make a leap of faith to accept even where we do not understand. Christ himself was not the finished Christ until he extended his arms on the cross and cried out, "Into your hands I commend my spirit!" As a half-finished Christ it takes humility to extend our arms in faith and say, "I'm ready, Lord. Choose me!"

CHAPTER TEN

The Mystery of Suffering

Joy! Let's start this chapter with joy. There is a flip side to suffering. God himself will dance with joy over our salvation. In Zephaniah 3:14–17 we read that God has repealed our sentence, which we incurred through Adam, and has taken away the evil we feared. God is in our midst, a victorious warrior. Yes, he will exalt over us and renew us by his love. He will dance with shouts of joy…for us. Wow! We shall end with joy, though we start with Adam's sentence in Genesis: "…by the sweat of your face you shall eat bread…and to dust you shall return."

Suffering and death are a part of the human condition. Original sin is the lack of original righteousness (justice) and holiness. The church has debated through the ages about original sin and redemption. Saint Paul said death is the effect of sin. Saint Augustine said original sin, our desire for sensual and material gratification, has been transferred to us by our parents. Karl Rahner, a contemporary theologian, says that Christ's death on the cross was to redeem all. As children of Adam we had sin, but as sons and daughters of God we have grace. We struggle with our tendency to sin and death, the effects of original sin, but they are only indications of a yet incomplete victory of grace. We must choose between "personal sin" and "faith, hope and charity." How we stand before God is determined by our "free choice," weakened though it is by our human nature.

In other words, whether we have heard about Christ or not, suffering and death are part of our existence. But Christ died for all of us and we all have the benefit of redemption. As we struggle with good and evil in our lives, we choose between sin and grace. We will be judged and rewarded for how we work for justice and love in the world. So we live with our human nature, our original sin history, and we struggle with the suffering and death that have been present since Adam and Eve. But we also live with the knowledge of redemption by the ongoing work of Christ, ever combating the effects of original sin in our world. And we die, ideally, surrendering our suffering and uniting it to the passion of Christ for the good and salvation of all. That is how our suffering is sanctified. That is how we follow Christ on the cross, moving toward Resurrection. Christ's sacrifice has redeemed all mankind, sanctifying all of our suffering and death, for all time. And that is why the heavens rejoice with a God who dances with shouts of joy, for us!

"What is there to sing about?" Penelope Cruz asks Nicholas Cage in the movie *Captain Corelli's Mandolin.* It is wartime in Greece. Cage and other soldiers are caught between Italian patriots and Axis invaders. Corelli (Cage) has an answer worth remembering. "There is singing when babies are baptized, when people get married, when soldiers march into battle. And there is singing when people die." The theme of despair and misery is always too close to the human condition. "Life is a comedy to those who think and a tragedy to those who feel." Somewhere between comic and tragic is where we strive to be, but we are never far from either extreme.

Let me illustrate with a light message I picked off the Internet recently: "I don't usually pass on sad news like this, but sometimes we need to pause and remember what life is all about. There was a great loss recently. Larry LaPrise, the Detroit native who wrote the song 'Hokey Pokey' died last week at the age of eighty-three. It was extremely difficult for the family to keep him in the casket. They'd put his left leg in and…well you know the rest." (My apologies to those who don't dance the hokey pokey.)

After a good belly laugh, we are ready to address the more serious issue of pain, despair and suffering. A simplistic inspiration, if that is not an oxymoron, struck me recently: How dark was the world before Christ? In the night of death, in the valley of darkness, Christ is our beacon. Actually, mankind was never wholly abandoned to evil and sin. God always wooed us through his prophets, and his angels are never far from us.

Another illustration comes to mind from popular TV fiction in a recent episode of *Touched by an Angel*. A prisoner about to be executed is the epitome of despair. His mother tries to see him and he refuses her pleas, telling her he will see her in hell. The background story is that the condemned man was abused by his father who frequently beat him with a belt, always giving him seven strokes. His mother kept count out loud. After the man kills his father and is on death row, an angel reveals to him that his mother had, in fact, helped him to the best of her ability. Her husband had been abused by his father who always administered twenty strokes. The mother pleaded with her husband, trying to take all the punishment on herself. He agreed to let her accept thirteen of the twenty strokes. In short, the condemned man accepts a final visit from his mother, is reconciled and asks her forgiveness.

You and I have a happier life and a happier end to look forward to. Christ took the strokes for our sins and died the death of a condemned criminal, all the while praying for those responsible. "The people who walked in darkness have seen a great light; those who lived in a land of deep shadows—on them light has shined" (Isaiah 9:2–4).

There is really no light side to suffering. If there were, could you buy a book that produces the opposite effect of a joke book? There is no such book. Besides, who would buy it? I do, however, know a few writers who could contribute to it.

At one point in my father-in-law's struggle to recover from a bypass operation I was feeling angry with God about the lack of progress. After one week and a number of setbacks, the doctors reintroduced a respiratory tube to breathe for him. I was really struggling with this turn of events. I was considering picketing the Chapel of Royal University Hospital in protest. In looking for answers to the mystery of suffering I turned to prayer. "The Birth of the Lord" in the joyful mysteries of the rosary reminded me that Christ was born and took on our flesh and our suffering to help us with this whole pain and death struggle. The realization that there is no Resurrection without a crucifixion still seemed trite and not consoling to me.

Suffering is part of the human condition and some of it is a direct result of our own free will. An existential explanation sounds intellectual, but it is really unsatisfying. Suffering has the face of a loved one. One of the most difficult moments I had as a parent was watching my infant suffering with fever. As you put your baby into a cool bath and listen to the heart-wrenching cries, you start to question the purpose of pain. At its deepest level, suffering is a mystery. Where there is suffering, Christ is close by. When the thief hung on the cross, Jesus said, "This day you will be with me in Paradise." Here we enjoy the emotional distance to recognize the Cross of Calvary as it applies to human suffering. It is a little harder to accept when a loved one is suffering.

God calls some of his dearest saints to share in Christ's suffering. My mother's wish was that she be part of this suffering at the time of her death. She did experience great pain and I saw it for what it was, wisdom in God's eyes, foolishness in the eyes of the world. Some of the greatest saints went joyfully to their torture and death.

A key aspect of suffering is communicated to us in Mark 8 when Jesus tells the disciples that he must undergo great suffering and be put to death. Saint Peter argues with Jesus about this. Jesus says, "Get behind me, Satan! For you are setting your mind not on divine things but on human things." Christ's suffering was for the salvation of all. Our suffering can be part of this salvation plan as we offer it for our sins and the redemption of all. My mother understood this concept and so did my Aunt Katie who offered up the suffering of many surgeries, "For the Holy Souls." In their simple faith my mother and aunt accepted "other world" values. I remember my aunt telling my mom after a funeral: "What a lovely funeral." I thought, "Yeah, right!" But as my mother-in-law says, you can't expect the wisdom of someone who is seventy-five to be found in someone who is fifty (thank goodness I'm over fifty).

I started this chapter on the lighter side, but there is seriousness to suffering. Ultimately we are called not only to accept our suffering but also to let Christ sanctify it. We can transcend suffering, go beyond it, by uniting it to the sacrifice of Christ. That is better than wasting it. Our greatest prayer is "Thy will be done." We do have some excellent examples to follow.

In *Much Ado About Nothing,* Shakespeare says: "There never was a philosopher that could bear a toothache patiently." When real pain hits us, such as the pain that often afflicts the dying, how do we reconcile this reality with the "very good" world God created? To people of faith the answer is simple. God, in his unfailing mercy, has provided a solution to the problem of man's sinful and rebellious nature. We will die as an effect of sin, but death will liberate us!

I once visited a man recovering from burns suffered in a propane explosion. All that could go wrong in the situation had gone wrong for him. After more than two months in intensive care, much of it in a coma, he was making gradual and painful progress.

We do not know why this accident happened. It is a simple solution to attribute it to our free will and human error—just an accident! But I learned something from the situation that suggests a much deeper meaning. I saw a human spirit that struggled to overcome despair and pain. I saw the fruits of many prayers and good wishes. Ultimately, I saw a spiritual grace at work in the acceptance of God's will. This grace touched all those who came in contact with the situation, including the young man.

What about the suffering involved with those who do not recover? The profound meaning of the cross is made known to us through suffering. Though we want it here and now, resurrection comes after death. The world looks to Christ's victory over death for meaning. All suffering and pain, just like all the troubles of this world, will vanish with our death and resurrection. What about taking up our cross on a daily basis? Nothing sounds less appealing than that invitation. Who would welcome suffering, pain and hardship? Yet it is the condition our flesh is heir to. Each of us knows deep down that we seek the Lord. For centuries the great writers and philosophers have been telling us that. If we have not tried to kill the feeling, we hunger for God. It is part of our human nature. Most of us have watched the drama of the cross and resurrection. Why can we not stay focused on the glory to come rather than on the hardships of this life?

Sometimes in this world God allows those most near and dear to His Son, like his saints, to partake more deeply of Christ's suffering. This is suffering that will remove the devastating effects of sin in our lives and in our world. The presence of the Holy Spirit can give us the vision to accept this, perhaps even to understand it. Ultimately our understanding is a matter of faith. Faith is a gift from God to us. It is something we should pray for and seek. It is also something we need to work with, to use. It will give us focus and give our journey purpose.

Imagine that you are invited to a great wedding feast. You know that it will take effort and time and sacrifice to get there. There is hardship involved, heavy traffic to go through. But it is easy to stay focused and committed. You know that it is all worth it, even the expense. How easy it is to make the effort when we are sure of the feast.

Jesus gave us a glimpse of heaven. He came to earth to reveal to us God's love. He has invited us to the eternal wedding feast. He is our invitation and our focus. How could we even think of not going to the banquet? The eternal heritage we look forward to makes our mundane, everyday tasks more tolerable. Faith can give our lives joy. One of the sayings of Jesus that emphasizes this cause for joy is: "Repent and believe in the Good News."

One invitation that challenges Christians is to ease the daily suffering of others in this world. Recently I had the experience of visiting three close friends in the hospital on the same day. Reflecting on their faith and particular stories brought me a little closer to God in the sense of the daily communion we should all be enjoying with our creator. The first patient I visited had endured much pain over the past week. This day's testing had not helped her condition much. "Why do I have this pain?" she was in effect asking. The most consoling thing I could think of was that with age comes pain and debilitation, and both of these are a sign that we are getting closer to God, literally. Her perspective included the deeper aspect of sharing in Christ's suffering. She pointed out that daily prayer was so great a part of her life that no matter what task she did, she was asking Jesus to bless her actions. Everything is a prayer.

I heard a theologian say recently, "Sometimes when I pray I am not conscious of it. 'Through him, with him, and in him...' is our every action." As brothers of Christ and sons of God, our actions, as we serve one another, are the actions of Jesus. Jesus himself tells the judges and us in John 10:34, "Is it not written in your law, 'I said, you are gods?'" And later in John 12:36 Jesus says, "...believe in the light, so that you may become children of light."

The second patient I visited had almost miraculously escaped a condition so serious that his doctor told him after the operation that he (his doctor) had little hope my friend would live. But prayer, a strong Polish constitution and some scar tissue from an earlier operation combined with the surgeon's special skill had brought success. When I approached my friend in his hospital bed, I found him deeply in prayer, communing with our Father. I enjoyed a cheerful and hope-filled visit and continued on my day's journey to the next patient. His story was somewhat different. He had been diagnosed with Alzheimer's disease. He had adjusted fairly well and, all things considered, seemed content to enjoy the good care and well-being of his new surroundings. He still enjoyed the jokes I shared with him. He held my hand for the last few minutes of our visit, and I gave him a blessing as I went. And so ended a typical visit with some of God's favorite children. It was giving, and it was receiving, and that is what we need to be for each other.

I continued my day's journey with a lighter heart and a realization that God is very close to us. We are not alone. And I thought of a song I had heard earlier in the morning, "What if God Was One of Us?" What if we journeyed through the day with him? We do. Not only that, but Christ journeys with us. We were not abandoned in our fallen state. The body of Christ nourishes us daily through the Eucharist and the Word to fortify us for the continuous struggle and sufferings in our lives.

First Corinthians 11:23–26 recalls the event of the Last Supper, an event we still celebrate today at every Christian Mass. The miracle of the multiplication of loaves and fishes (Luke 9:16–17) is symbolic of the power and miracle of the Eucharist. Bread is broken, is multiplied; the Body of Christ, broken, is multiplied. Christ's body, broken, becomes more, becomes enough to nourish the whole of mankind. At every moment somewhere on this earth, Mass is being celebrated; Jesus is offering himself to the Father on our behalf as he did on the Cross and at the Last Supper. Christ's body, broken, is enough to nourish all of us, spiritually, for all time.

The "bread of life" is good news for us. Jesus said whoever eats this bread will have life everlasting and will be raised up on the last day. In John 6:51 Jesus says: "I am the living bread that came down from heaven. Whoever eats of this bread will live forever." This was a difficult concept for Jesus' followers to accept. Throughout John 6 Jesus says several times and in different ways: "Those who eat my flesh and drink my blood abide in me and I in them."

The power of Jesus living in us has a very positive effect on us. How can we be anything but energized into loving others? I'd like to share one experience of this I had during the time I was helping out at the hospital during a strike. When I came home one night, I felt I had been at a holy place. The patients there were just that—patients—waiting patiently for love and care from us, and in a deeper sense, waiting for God's love. Feeding them and caring for them is tending the body of Christ. The experience of working in the lodge during the strike was very spiritual. The chance to really feed and clothe the living, suffering body of Christ is a profound experience.

But the situation at the hospital made this an artificial experience in some ways. You and I get the chance every day to tend to others: to feed and clean, to care for them, to do the dishes, to clean a room or do the laundry. Somehow we don't always rise to the unheroic challenges of everyday living. But it is still there, the challenge to serve others. "Do you really love me?" Jesus asked Peter three times. "Then feed my lambs," he said; "Feed my sheep." Elsewhere Jesus says, "In as much as you have done this for the least of my brothers and sisters, you have done it for me."

In another real life situation, a pilgrimage to Our Lady of Lourdes at Rama, Saskatchewan, I had the opportunity to observe a pilgrim who sat in the pew, outdoors, long after most had sought the warmth of the nearby hall and lunch and coffee. The final hour of this night's meditation was a very chilly one. I felt that perhaps some of us were stuck there because we were too frozen to move. Then, in reflection, I realized a certain worshipful acceptance on the part of this man with the crutches. He just sat there in silent communion, in a prayerful pose, with his Lord. There was a reflection of creator and creature. Then I realized another truth in God's scheme of things: They also serve who only sit and wait.

I would like to conclude this chapter with a story related to suffering. Everyone loves a great story. That's why Jesus told so many. It was a tradition of every wise rabbi. The story I want to share is related to a quote from Malachi 3: "He will sit as a refiner and purifier of silver."

This verse puzzled some ladies in a Bible study class, so they tried to discover its meaning. One of the ladies visited a silversmith and watched him at work. He held a piece of silver over the fire and heated it. He explained that to refine silver you need to hold it over the hottest part of the fire so it would burn away all the impurities. The woman thought about us and how God might hold us in such a hot spot: "He sits as a refiner and purifier of silver." She asked the artisan if it was true he had to sit there in front of the fire the whole time the silver was being purified. He not only said yes, but he explained that he had to keep his eyes on that silver the whole time. If the silver stayed in the fire too long, it would be destroyed. The woman reflected for a moment then asked, "How do you know when the silver is fully refined?" "When I can see my image in it," he replied.

How does this story apply to real life? The best example I can think of is my father-in-law. My father-in-law Walter grew closer to the Lord in his later years. In his youth he had had some rough edges, as we all do, but the Lord led him on a sure path. As a grandfather to my children, he was kind, gentle and generous. He was the image of our heavenly father in many ways. He was patient and prayerful, always there for the convocations or marriages of his grandchildren, even when he could scarcely walk the required steps or drive the many kilometers.

When he went into the hospital that final time for his heart operation, he was aware of the Jerusalem he might be entering. He asked us the morning of his operation, "Would anyone like to trade places with me?" After his operation I felt like Saint Peter looking at the coming sufferings of Christ in Jerusalem, "This must not happen to you" (Matthew 16:22). If he was to die, I preferred a quiet passing before he recovered from the anesthetic.

But the Lord had a greater plan in mind. The sufferings of the next month concluded with the refiner's fire of the last hours of Walter's life. We knew he was already in the Lord's hands and that we could see Christ's image in Walter's suffering. I realized that his suffering and agony were part of a larger plan—they were united to the suffering of Christ which redeems us all. In the end all we could do was say "Amen." I did try to sing a few alleluias through my tears.

CHAPTER ELEVEN

In Loving Arms

I want to start this chapter with two illustrations about what it means to be in the circle of loving arms. The first story is one from nature. A cougar was attempting to attack a bear cub that climbed a tree to escape. The tree branch broke, dumping the cub into moving waters. The cub scrambled to get aboard a drifting log which was being washed toward a not-too-distant waterfall. The cougar, biding its time, ran alongside the torrent toward the waterfall so it could pick off the cub. As the cub neared the waiting cougar, it had to jump into the water to prevent attack. As it floundered in the water, the cub whimpered with a heart-rending cry, inevitably having to scramble to solid ground towards which the cougar was bounding.

What ensued was heart-wrenching. The cub made a feeble attempt to stand up to the cougar which attacked the nose and head of the cub. The cub's pleas sounded not unlike that of a child's, pleading for help. Above all this there suddenly began a roaring and rending sound that paralyzed the cougar, stopping it cold. The mother grizzly bear came storming on to the scene, causing the cougar to flee in no uncertain terms. The indignant mother stood and roared ferociously for several moments while the cub scrambled toward the heart-warming reunion.

The grizzly slobbered a salivary bath over the wounded face. The sounds of happy reunion and reassurance of continued future protection were absolute. A later camera shot showed the baby grizzly snuggling up to the mother in the den, preparing to sleep. Tiny paws reached out to the sheltering protection, touching the huge paws, and the tiny nose snuggled within the range of protection.

As much as the grizzly showed absolute concern for its cub, we have a deep knowledge that our heavenly Father's love is more perfect. When we "snuggle" closer to God in our meditation or prayer, we can be sure that as we reach out to touch God, that the hand of God is around us. If we cry for help as a child of God, God's care and response is sure and immediate.

The second introductory example I want to share is from a Christmas story by Richard Ryan. In a true story by Ryan, he is conversing with a vagrant, and after striking up a short friendship he asks the vagrant, "How long has it been since someone hugged you?" "A long time," he replied. And so they embrace in the rain as they say goodbye. How long has it been since an old person living near you has been hugged? The single person? The widowed? The teen?

I experienced just such an embrace last Christmas. For some time I had been visiting an elderly widow who was struggling to live alone. Inspired by Ryan's story, I gave her a warm hug when I delivered my Christmas package. It was a powerful moment and there were tears. Hugs are free! There should be more of them. The embrace of our heavenly Father is also free. All we need to do is take a moment to put ourselves there.

ABBA

When I was a teen in high school, in the fall of the year, my after-school job on the farm was to round up the cattle and make sure they did not stray too far from our land, which was not fenced at the time. As I rode on horseback bringing the milk cows home, I used to notice how the sun shining on the stubble field reflected more brightly on the ends of the stubble on one spot that used to follow along beside me, almost like a silhouette, as I rode through the field. I used to imagine that this glow or halo that followed me was a sign of how important I was to God and how special and privileged I was. Just being in the saddle on a mount already made me feel like privileged gentry of a bygone age. Well, my perception was not even close to the truth. I repeat, not even close to the truth of how privileged you and I are, and how special we are in the eyes of God our Creator.

God was guiding me then, as he is now, guiding my growth. Isaiah 40:11 tells us, "He will feed his flock like a shepherd; he will gather the lambs in his arms, and carry them in his bosom." Isaiah 42:6 continues, "I am the LORD, I have called you in righteousness, I have taken you by the hand and kept you." Truly we are in God's hands. Our every breath is his continued gift to us.

God is much closer to us and loves us more profoundly than my youthful imagination could perceive. Let me use an example to illustrate: picture a little boy slipping into his daddy's shoes, putting on his dad's oversized gloves and hat, strutting along saying, "I am daddy!" This child is probably aware that his father has affection for him. But does he know what is really in his father's mind as he watches his child: "You little snapper! If only you knew how proud I am of you! How much I love you. Every little gesture of your hand, the way you swing your foot. Do you know how long I've loved you and what plans I have for your future? You will be great! I will give you everything I have. I will watch over you. You're just too much for words."

Do you think our heavenly Father's capacity for love of his children is any less than that of an earthly father? It was Jesus who showed us the way to the Father's heart when he referred to his father as "Abba" or "Daddy!" The heart of Jesus is perhaps closer to us than the heart of God our Father. One of the pictures that filled my childhood years with wonder and is still sold to tourists at holy sites around the world is the image of Christ, with a heart superimposed on his chest, a picture that depicts the sacred love of Christ for us. Perhaps at times we have almost resented the prominence of this image that has been an idol for tourists and a reminder of the childhood piety we turned our backs on as enlightened teenagers.

The image of the Sacred Heart of Jesus is worthy of a revisit and meditation. In John 19:31–37 we read of the heart of Jesus pierced with a lance. Having watched this reenacted in the Passion Play and having heard it proclaimed in the Gospels for some fifty years, I still was missing some of the essential meaning of the scene. In the witness of the centurion on the scene we become aware of the profound connection between Christ's divine life and his humanity:

"...and at once blood and water came out." In John's account blood and water *gushed* out. How could something "gush" from so depleted and exhausted a body? It was Jesus' burning love for us! "He who saw this has testified so that you may believe." Even in death, Jesus poured out all he had: his blood to atone for our sins, taking the punishment for them; and water pouring out as the baptismal water that cleanses us of sin.

As I reflect on this image of the Sacred Heart today, I see much more than I did as a child or a teenager. The absolute, unlimited and unconditional love of Christ on the cross can change our lives. He loved us before we were born. He opened up his arms on the Cross; his embrace is still open. He still loves us in spite of our foolish sins. And he gave more than was humanly possible even after his death when the soldiers pierced his heart with a lance.

IN LOVING ARMS

A couple of summers ago I was put in touch with the role of the church in a very dramatic way. I experienced the arms of a loving Christ on the occasion of a funeral for my nephew who was killed in a motorcycle accident. Talk about a challenge! What do you say when life ends at thirty-six? The role of the church in this situation is to bring the hope and consolation of Christ's message to the people.

The minister at the service, my brother Ron, pointed out how at birth this young man was put into the gentle hands of a loving mother, our sister Leona. But after his death, this same man was born into a new life with hands that received him in a more perfect love and gentleness. Before birth we leave the living energy which is God. This was our first home, our first love, before birth. At death we move back to the heart of God.

The experience of the funeral brought home to me in a deep way the tremendous role of the church. The church is the loving arms of Christ on earth. Mother church warmly shelters and consoles us during such a sad time. She welcomes us back from our sometimes errant ways. If we really understood Christ's work through his church, the pews would be filled on Sunday mornings. Christ speaks to us in the

Word. He wants to touch us physically in the Eucharist. Sometimes we only make that encounter possible on rare occasions like funerals and weddings.

One of the most consoling sounds we can ever hear is the words, "Come to me." There is a heartrending scene in *The Miracle Worker* where the mother Kate Keller has been separated from her child for a whole week so Annie Sullivan could try to make some progress teaching a blind and deaf Helen Keller. Finally the week is up and Kate cannot stand it a minute longer. She cries out, "Let her come to me!"

Jesus wants us as desperately as a mother wants her child. His words, "Come to me, all you that are weary and are carrying heavy burdens, and I will give you rest" (Matthew 11:28) express Christ's absolute longing for us. He wants us all, sinners and righteous; and we all qualify. As a parent I have had to watch children leave home, with tears, to go off to university or out into the work world. With the love of a parent I've had to reflect, "This is good for you. It will make you strong. But you go with my love." In the same way, God's love, the Holy Spirit, is with us to make us strong. If Christ had not left, that love could not have been here in the person of the Holy Spirit. Jesus calls to us, "Come to me!" He calls us more than once. Three times Jesus called to Simon Peter and asked Peter, "Do you love me?" (John 21:15–17). Jesus longs for us everyday. Our lives become crowded with our fears, distractions and secular pursuits. We need to pause occasionally to listen, to let the Holy Spirit move us to hear the call of Jesus, "Come to me!"

Just as surely as a parent phones to check on a child who has left home, Jesus is calling to us to check how we are, to ask us to lay down our burden, to make it lighter. I have known parents (more than one) who have called their son or daughter every night for months, literally, to check how they were doing or how their day was. Our heavenly Father certainly has as much concern for us, and has a more perfect love for us. If only we could believe it! If only we could learn to listen daily, we would hear, "Come to me!"

As parents we get to experience the loving concern and devotion our heavenly Father most surely feels for us. From the moment of the conception of our first child, my wife and I became parents. I remember going to prenatal classes on parenting. It is something we took seriously. Both of us had university classes in psychology and sociology, and I had classes on childhood ranging from anthropology to behavioral psychology. We took this new role of parenting seriously. Our heavenly Father is a perfect parent and knows all about us: our struggles, our successes and failures, and our motivations. Fear not.

Recently I came across a metaphor from real life that should give us confidence and security in our relationship with our heavenly Father. My son was swimming in a triathlon event at Waskesui on the weekend. The waters were choppy with whitecaps. His usual twenty-eight-minute mile became forty-two minutes. At times he felt he had to give up because he couldn't get his breath in the frigid water. And while this was going on, my wife and I were at Sunday services praying for him and commiserating with his struggle. Our hearts were with him and we waited anxiously for his return.

Just as my son fought with the waves on what should have been an easier swim, being tossed back and having to struggle through the buffeting waves, so we too at times struggle through life's difficulties. We seemingly make progress but are borne back by the forces which seem to overwhelm us. Yet we know our heavenly father is there for us, watching over us, giving us the graces we need to continue on to reach that goal which at times seems to be eluding us. Fear not.

There is more good news. Our God, like a good parent, enjoys taking the time to teach us and train us, and he even finds ways to have fun with us. God gives us many pleasures. The spiritual joys, the physical and sensual pleasures of life—yes, especially these, he created for us to enjoy. There is an old Jewish proverb which says: "Any one who sees a legitimate pleasure and does not enjoy it is an ingrate against God who made it possible."

Fear not. God created us out of love and wants to share heaven with us. He wants us to subdue the earth (his gifts) and conquer it. His delight is in our enjoyment of the wonderful gifts of his creation. He does not focus on our faults, but has given the life of his very own son to make heaven a reality for us. An understanding of God's great love for us will drive us through the buffeting waves toward that distant shore, where he waits anxiously with open arms.

I would like to share one more example about the loving arms of our father before I leave this section of Chapter 11. A couple of years ago I attended a weekend workshop in Regina, and at the closing liturgy on Saturday afternoon I was struck by a familiar image of love. I purposely chose the word "familiar" because it involved a family who was doubtless tired from the challenges such a socially interactive weekend demands. The father of the family was seated with his arm wrapped about his daughter who was perhaps eleven years old. Her feet were sprawling in relaxation, and her ponytail rested on her father's shoulder. And it struck me that for the moment all the struggles and tensions, all the worries of growing up in a school and peer group, that all these tensions were at bay, and that this child was resting in security.

Then I reflected that just in this way a spouse should be able to lie in the arms of his or her mate and be completely secure and at rest. It is only from that kind of security that we are enabled to "launch out into the deep," as Jesus calls us to go into the service of each other in our everyday activities. And then I reflected a little deeper and realized that we really need to put ourselves into the arms of God our father whenever the struggles and pressures of life become overbearing. "Come to me, all you that are weary and carrying heavy burdens, and I will give you rest." All too frequently we need to "unburden" ourselves, to ask God's help so we can get through the day or the night. If you have been carrying something for several hours, it is time! It is time to put it into the hands of the Lord. Your problems won't automatically disappear, but rest assured, you will find solace. Your burden will be lighter. God will give you a break from the tensions you have been under.

At a very low point in his Montgomery struggle, one night when his very life had just been threatened, Martin Luther King prayed to God, "I have nothing left. I've come to the point where I can't face it alone." At that moment, in his own words, "I experienced the presence of the Divine as I had never experienced him before"[i]

"Come to me, all you that are weary and carrying heavy burdens, and I will give you rest" (Matthew 11:28–29).

REACHING OUT TO OTHERS

The story is told of a church that was bombed during the Second World War. Among the ruins stood a statue of Christ with both arms missing. Someone had hung a sign around the neck of the statue on which was written, "I have no hands but your hands." Just as Christ extended his arms on the cross, we need to extend our arms to others we meet on our journey to God.

How often have you seen a sign reading "John 3:16" at a televised football game or sports event? The camera always finds this sign and makes a brief focus. John 3:16 is the message of salvation history in a nutshell: "For God so loved the world that he gave his only Son, so that everyone who believes in him may not perish but may have eternal life." Can it be so simple? The bigger question is do we believe? Have we given our lives to God in faith? The lure of the flesh—money, power, the things of this world—is very strong. We struggle. That is why we need the cross of Christ.

Just as the Hebrews held up a serpent in the wilderness, and all who looked on it were saved from the poisonous serpents; so the cross is lifted up, and all who look in faith on the crucified Christ will be saved. Of our own merits, we cannot be saved. We need to trust in the love of Christ who died to redeem the sinner. Remember what Karl Rahner said: "Most of the time when we sin, we do know what we are doing, but we don't know how much God loves us—hence we are still innocent through ignorance."

If we have faith in God, not only will we be saved and created anew, but our very sins will be forgotten. In Isaiah 65 we hear:

> For I am about to create new heavens
>   and a new earth;
> the former things shall not be remembered
>   or come to mind.
> But be glad and rejoice forever
>   in what I am creating:

for I am about to create Jerusalem as a joy,
   and its people as a delight.
I will rejoice in Jerusalem,
   and delight in my people;
no more shall the sound of weeping be heard in it,
   or the cry of distress.

God will create us anew. Our sins will not be remembered.

We have explored the loving arms of our father, and we have explored the eternally open arms of Christ our brother, but as we know from childhood, so many times when we need someone to intercede with "Dad," we could turn to the soft heart of our mother. I know from personal experience that our mother Mary will answer our prayers if doing so is good for our salvation. So many stories come to mind. I will mention one that left a deep impression on me as a child.

A neighbor of ours had been struggling with lung cancer for several years. Sometimes he made progress, and then it appeared he was losing the battle. He made a pilgrimage to pray at the shrine of Mary at Cape-Du-Madeleine in Quebec. He asked her, simply, "Either cure me or take me." He returned to the farm from his trip. A short time later he fell ill. Within the same day he was taken to the hospital, received the sacraments of Reconciliation and Holy Communion as well as the Anointing of the Sick and died rather peacefully.

My articles on Mary, the Mother of Christ, have sometimes prompted critical response from some readers who do not share my Roman Catholic theology of Mary, so I will add something on the lighter side. The story is told of the Holy Family chatting about revisiting earth. Saint Peter asked them what places they'd like to visit. Jesus said he'd like to visit Nazareth, see the old carpenter shop. It had many memories. Joseph said he'd like to visit Egypt, since he spent such a short time there and traveled at night. Mary said, "I'd like to visit Medjugorje. I've never really been there."

What do you really know about Mary? What is your relationship with her? If you are not close to Mary, you are missing one of the great loves of your life!

To me, Mary is a mother. She experienced human pain and suffering. She watched her son die on the cross. There was pain and there was mystery. Mary pondered the mysteries of salvation in her heart. Mary was chosen to be the mother of Jesus. She accepted, though she was an unwed mother in danger of being stoned to death. She went through the nativity and all the physical and psychological hardships of giving birth to her firstborn in a stable. Then there was the flight into Egypt, losing Jesus in the temple visit, the beheading of John the Baptist, and pondering all the while about where this son of hers was heading.

Mary is our spiritual mother. God bestowed on her the greatest honor, the conception of the messiah in her womb and the birth of his son Jesus. Her life was free from sin. Death was not allowed to decay her body. She was raised into heaven, body and soul. How is Mary our spiritual mother? Theologically, we are baptized into the life of Christ. That makes us brothers with Mary's son. She loves us as her children. When Christ was dying he saw Mary and the disciple John at the foot of the cross. Jesus said to Mary, "Woman, this is your son." And to the disciple he said, "Here is your mother" (John 19:26). Today we are those disciples at the foot of the cross. Jesus is our brother through Baptism, and Mary is our mother as much as she was the mother of John. If we are not aware of this relationship, we are missing a great love in our lives.

When a woman experiences motherhood, feeling the baby move in her womb, she loves her child and enjoys an intimate closeness that words cannot describe. Her dreams and aspirations for that child are profound. I realize here that I am merely a man trying to describe what a woman experiences in a situation too profound for words. But catch the emotion, the connection. That is how Mary loves us, her children.

In her many apparitions on earth, like Fatima and Lourdes, or more recently Medjugorje, Mary tries to draw us back to God. She shows a profound concern for peace on earth, for her children. And she pleads with us to pray! I realize that not everyone believes in the apparitions of Mary, but the leap of faith here is not that difficult. If we believe in the Incarnation of Christ, the Resurrection, and many of the other events surrounding Jesus Christ, why would it be difficult to realize that Mary still plays a vital role and is concerned about our personal salvation?

I have called on Mary many times in my life, especially when I needed a mother of grace. In the angst of youth I remember praying especially faithfully to Mary. One year when the Pope declared a Holy Year we were encouraged to pray the complete rosary every day for that year. The "complete rosary," for those who don't know, consisted then of fifteen decades (ten "Hail Marys") rather than the usual five decades. I managed to maintain that rigorous spiritual exercise for the year. The reason I mention it is that many of my deepest prayers of youth were answered. For example, I prayed to Mary that I would meet a suitable helpmate whom I could love and have a family with. In the fullness of time that prayer was answered in the wife I have loved for more than thirty years now.

I have also been fortunate to know the love of my mother, before she died thirty years ago. At times I still feel as close to her as I did "when I was being made in secret, / intricately woven" in her womb (Psalm 139:15). And for some thirty years I have been privileged to know the love of a mother-in-law, the grandmother of my children. It is only fitting that we also enjoy a closeness to our heavenly mother Mary.

NOTES

i Martin Luther King, Jr., *Stride Toward Freedom: The Montgomery Story* (New York: HarperCollins, 1987).

CHAPTER TWELVE

Marriage and Family

An old joke relates how duct tape is like "the force." It has a dark side and a light side, and it holds the universe together. Love is the force. It holds a couple together and it holds a family together. The need for love and reconciliation in families is illustrated in this story:

> In a small town in Spain a man named Jorge had a bitter argument with his son Paco. That night Paco ran away from home. Jorge's love for Paco drove him to post a huge sign in the town square which read, "Paco, come home. I love you. Meet me here tomorrow morning." Next morning when Jorge arrived there were seven young men named Paco, each hoping it was his dad waiting with open arms.[i]

It is good that we experience human love in this life; it is a foretaste of the divine love which we will have to a greater degree in heaven. We already know that God loves us. Jesus says in John 16:27, "The Father himself loves you." He loves us as he loved Jesus. Jesus said, "I have made your name known to them [us]...so that the love with which you loved me may be in them, and I in them" (John 17:26).

It is amazing what a transforming power love has. Let me illustrate. A married couple was struggling in their relationship and each was feeling shortchanged in love. They started keeping notes on what the other had said or done. The realization of what was happening to their love led one of them to reflect on the Lord's love and forgiveness. The last entry in the journal read: "Forgive us our trespasses as we forgive those who trespass against us...I love you. I love you. I love you!"

"Love covers a multitude of sins" (1 Peter 4:8); it transforms us! Let me illustrate with one more example. A third-grader named Tommy had behavior problems in school because his parents had recently separated. The teacher contrived to have both parents attend an interview, each not knowing the other was going to be there. The situation was a little icy. Silently the teacher took a piece of paper she had found crumpled in Tommy's desk and handed it to the mother. After she read it, she handed it to her husband without a word. His frown softened as he read. He studied it for what seemed an eternity. Then he folded it carefully, placed it in his pocket, and reached for his wife's outstretched hand. She wiped her eyes and smiled. They left together. The words on the sheet of yellow paper simply said: "Dear Mother...Dear Daddy...I love you...I love you...I love you."[ii]

MARRIAGE

Summer is the season for weddings. Marriage is that occasion when actions that were formerly forbidden suddenly become compulsory (as Hal Roach once said). If you have ever been in love, you know the depth of feeling, the passion. You would be willing to give your life for your lover. Just hold that thought!

As another summer of weddings unfolds, young couples look to society for blessing and support as they embark on a central part of their life's vocation. The church is still called upon for its blessing in many marriages. And marriage still has a mystery about it— something sacred, like a sacrament. Marriage is a sacrament; though as Thornton Wilder tells us in *Our Town,* not everyone is sure what that means. It means that if God is a partner in your marriage, you can call for help when you need it. A sacrament has special graces attached to it. And when you need those graces or that help, God will honor his part of the bargain. All you need to do is ask. I speak from the experience of thirty-some years of marriage. Whenever my wife and I asked for help (I should say when we were desperate and demanded help), we received it. Sometimes we struggled because we were giving less than the one hundred percent God is always ready to give.

In the play *Our Town* Thornton Wilder, the stage manager, says to the audience that "m" marries "n." There are many marriages. Once in 10,000 times it is interesting. Behind the apparent callous remark about the insignificance of the 9,999 marriages, there is a special message for the one in 10,000. I would even go farther and say one in a million. If you are not prepared to make your marriage one in a million, it won't be.

The secret to a successful marriage is commitment. If you are prepared to go fifty-fifty with your partner, it will be a struggle. You will always be fighting about the borderline. If you are prepared to give sixty percent or one hundred percent, your odds for a great marriage go up proportionally. If both parties to a marriage attempt to give one hundred percent, not only will their marriage be great, but society will benefit. Their children will be blessed and so will their community. There will be so much love and care flowing from this union. You do the math.

Before I leave this introduction to the chapter I want to throw out a challenge to couples in a marriage. On a record-breaking hot day in August I noticed how one person or two, sleeping in a bedroom at night in the absence of air-conditioning, can give off enough heat to change the temperature of the room. A finite energy source, like the sexual energy of a stripper in a bar, can affect a room filled with people. Imagine how profoundly our spiritual energy, which is infinite, can affect others around us. We have all seen how one person, like a spirited evangelist, can give off a presence of Christ that can transform thousands of people. Imagine what two people, like a married couple for example, can do to influence the world in a positive and powerful way. We are not all gifted evangelists, but we do all have a spiritual essence. Sometimes the mere presence of a person can leave a profound and lasting impression on others.

FAMILY

As humans we must confess certain inadequacies and point to the perfect love of God our Father. It is important that we as earthly fathers and mothers reflect, even in a small measure, the unconditional love that God has for his children.

The year 1999 was celebrated by the Roman Catholic Church as the year of God the Father. This was a special year to explore the concept of God as Father. As earthly fathers I believe we can assert a certain prerogative to help our families understand the love of fathers for their children. In 1999 I sent each of my children a special note listing what I saw as some of their special gifts and expressing the love and support that will always be there for them. Membership in a family begins with that sacred bond that is established when you first hold your child in your hands. This family bond also binds children. As a youth attending university I remember writing a letter to my parents thanking them for their gift of life, their heroic sacrifices and their love. These were not the words I used, but they were certainly the message. This was by now a family tradition, since I remember the joy similar letters from my older brothers and sisters had brought my parents.

The concept of God as Father has been questioned in recent years. Even leading theologians are writing about God as Mother. Recently I came across an article making the case for God the Father as *Father*. Jesus was very definite about the use of the term Father, as was God the Father on the occasion of the Baptism of Jesus when the voice from heaven said, "This is my Son, the Beloved, with whom I am well pleased" (Matthew 3:17). As well, Jesus was very clear in telling us about our heavenly Mother Mary. From the agony of the cross he spoke to Mary and indicating John, the beloved disciple, he said, "Woman, this is your son." Then to John he said, "This is your mother." Traditionally Mary has been accorded the role of our mother, the mother of the church, since all grace flows to us through her role as Mother of Christ.

Observing the year of the Father in 1999 reminded every father on earth to seriously reflect on his sacred role. It is a reminder to grow in understanding of fatherhood in the temporal and eternal sense, a reminder to herald the love of God the Father for all his children. Fatherhood and motherhood are so important in our society that we have instituted a special day to celebrate each. Let us consider the significance of these days in turn.

A few thoughts come to mind as I pause to reflect on Mother's Day. I am led to reflect on my own mother, as I hope you will reflect on yours. My mother lived her life ten miles from the hamlet of Cactus Lake. She spent all her years hidden, in a sense, from the parade of public view. She struggled with poverty, drought and dirty diapers. Yet in God's salvation plan she is still shining and her work still goes on. In those quiet years she passed on values at the kitchen table, in the family rosary circle each night, and on Sunday morning on our way to church when she checked our ears to be sure the prairie dust was indeed washed off.

Today my mother still lives in her children. What is best in us we picked up from her and from my father. Mom always wanted four priests from her eight sons (and she wasn't even Irish). She had to settle for two, so far, but she didn't envision the changing church. At least five other children are lay presiders; another is a nun. Her oldest son finished his lay presider training this past year, after he retired from the workplace.

Robert Frost, in his poem "Death of A Hired Man" says, "Home is the place where, when you have to go there, they have to take you in." Your mother is the one who first loved you unconditionally, before you were born. Only God has loved you longer.

Your mother is the one who prays for you when you have a test, when you are starting a new job or when she cannot reach to help you.

In elementary school I learned a little poem about Mother's Day. "*M* is for the Million things she gave me": like the nose wipes, like all the big changes in the first two years of my life, like all the diapers hung out in winter to "freeze dry" in the days before electricity, like checking our ears just as we were leaving for church to be sure the Saturday baths had reached there.

My mother will never grow old. She died in her mid-fifties, but she died a happy death. She asked God to let her suffer. Her last days were extremely painful—pain that she united to the suffering of Christ and offered for our sins. Our awareness of this suffering was her gift to us. My wife and I were privileged to be close to her in the last days and to see a smile touch her face when she perceived our presence. I am reminded of a precious gift that several sons gave their mother as she lay dying in hospital. They sang her favorite church hymns as she went through the valley of darkness and into eternal light. They sang their mother into heaven.

I hope you can finish the poem "M is for…" with thoughts about your mother. If you are privileged to still have a mother on earth, give her a hug, a bouquet, a visit. She has given you life! Reflect on everything else she has given you. If you are like me, and your mother has gone to her reward, pause for a moment. Close your eyes and cross your arms over your chest. Enjoy her presence and her embrace for a little while. She still loves you.

Your heavenly mother Mary is also there for you. She knows about suffering, having to watch her son crucified. Ask her for special intercessions, favors. She answers prayers with the heart of a mother.

In most societies there is no single word that evokes more emotion, recognition, reflection or deeper connotation than the word *mother*, except perhaps the word *father*. The father is the creator, maker, sustainer and the list goes on. The traditional role of king and warrior is harder to recognize in the nuclear family of today, but it is still there and it is important. So is the role of lover. It is a challenge to bring the concept of father down from high Olympus, literally, where Zeus dwelled, to a farm ten miles from Cactus Lake, Saskatchewan, where I first saw what a father was.

In a note to my parents I composed sometime in the past year I said: "Thank you for providing a place secure enough for me to grow, open enough for my imagination, and restful enough when I needed rest. And thank you for the inspiration, the example. All these things I can never repay you for. The best thing I can hope to do is to follow your example." My parents passed on to their eternal reward twenty-seven years ago, but I am closer to them now than I was as a child.

There is a mystery in the role of being a father or a mother. It is only possible when that unique condition exists that is called a child. To illustrate this in flesh and blood I will refer to a movie called *Replacing Dad*. There is a special place in the heart that only a child's love can touch. *Replacing Dad* tells a story of a father of two children who leaves his wife for a mistress. Eventually she too leaves him and he is so lost he plans to kill himself. In a desperate move he calls his wife. She enters the motel room and is trying to get him to put down the gun. She fails.

Enter the children, a teenage boy and a daughter about eight. There is a place in the father's heart that only the love of a child can reach. In a heartwrenching scene the children succeed where the adults were helpless. Children are precious, irreplaceable. With hindsight, which is usually 20/20, we can see how our parents must have loved us. Perhaps we were not perfect in that relationship; perhaps they were not perfect. But one thing is certain; our heavenly father's love for us is perfect. Again, I invite the reader to take a moment with your father, if he has passed on, or with your heavenly father. Close your eyes. Be present with your father. Rest there for a while.

The biggest failure in our relationship with God our Father is that we do not understand how much he loves us. Jesus tried so many different ways to show us the father's love for us. The shepherd calls his sheep. The prodigal son is welcomed with open arms. Perhaps we are like a son or daughter who has been in the father's house all these years but just never realized the intimacy of love. God is a lover, a creator, a king, a sustainer. We have a special relationship with him that allows us to touch his heart as only a child can. There is a special place in God's heart that only a child's love can reach. We are closer to the heart of our God than we can ever realize in this world. "I have loved you with an everlasting love; therefore I have continued my faithfulness to you" (Jeremiah 31:3).

As a father in a family I once wrote a letter to my children to encourage them in their struggle to be good family members in the family of God and in the family that is the church. I quote it in its entirety for the reader:

LETTER TO MY CHILDREN
I remember driving to church one evening when the sunset was heavenly. I observed to my teenaged son how this scene reflected the touch of God. He didn't seem impressed. I realized at the time that he was at that age when many have a natural allergy to talk of God and religious things. Now I address this article to you as young adults.

You are still not as excited about God and religion as I am, and that is natural. But as adults we should be aware of the reality that escaped us in our carefree youth. What exactly do you miss if you do not go to church Sunday morning?

Let us think of a marriage. A man and woman pledge their fidelity to each other and promise to be loving and faithful. Suppose they felt that they had a healthy relationship and they did not really need special time together or physical intimacy on a regular basis. "We love each other. That should be enough to keep us this week, this month…" How long would this marriage be great, even if it could last?

Sunday, and any day that you can attend a Eucharistic service, you are renewing your spiritual life, that intimacy that Christ established through his church. Yes, the Sacrament of Bread and Wine is a physical union, a touching in a sensual way, of that love between Christ and his church. I know this is a difficult concept for many, even shocking, as it was in the time of Christ when many turned away from him because of his words (John 6:51–71). But it is as true today as it was at that intimate scene of the Last Supper. God wants to touch us and be close to us in love.

To my married children I emphasize these thoughts. One absolute and central bond my wife and I share is our faith. Doubtless, as you probably can remember, your parents went through times of disagreement and misunderstanding. But one guarantee our family always enjoyed was that on Sunday morning Mom and Dad stood before the altar of God and exchanged a sign of peace. And more important, we were united in that banquet of Love that is the Eucharist. Whatever our problems, and I won't list them here, you knew that we were one in church on Sunday morning.

Just as a husband and wife need to be one in a marriage, and need to nurture that meeting of minds with a physical intimacy to keep their marriage strong, so we need to nurture our union with Christ. We need his frequent touch, and for that reason Jesus instituted the church and left the sacraments to nourish us regularly. Small wonder that one of the first commandments God gave us is to "keep holy the Sabbath Day."

Sometimes the church that you belong to finds it difficult to talk about shockingly intimate and sensual physical union. And perhaps that is one reason the meaning of our union with Christ in the sacraments has not been passed on effectively to younger members of the church. But it is our human need to communicate intimacy by touching in the flesh. That is why Christ left us the sacrament we touch and taste with our tongues. My parting wish is that when you look at your parents and your church you will continue to see members who "talk the talk" and "walk the walk."

— ‡ —

As parents we struggle with the task God has given us to evangelize our families, our parish community and our world. As a catechist for several decades I used to worry about how successful I could be at teaching students about Jesus when some parents were so indifferent they did not attend church services. Finally I came across the answer to my worries in Isaiah 55:10–11:

> as the rain and the snow come down from heaven,
> > and do not return there until they have watered the
> > earth,
> making it bring forth and sprout,
> > giving seed to the sower and bread to the eater,
> *so shall my word* be that goes out from my mouth;
> > it shall not return to me empty, but it shall
> > > accomplish that which I purpose,
> > > and succeed in the thing for which I sent it.
> (Emphasis added)

The parable Jesus uses to explain how the Word of the Kingdom is planted as a seed and grows or does not grow (Matthew 13) further clarified my role as a catechist. I was a sower, scattering the seed of God's word. God's promise is that his word will bear fruit in time and in eternity.

As a parent I find great consolation in the words from Isaiah. Often parents worry as their children go through a time of soul-searching when they may actually stop attending church services. The

Word of God has been planted and will in time bear the fruit it is meant to. Only God knows the time and the place. I know of one young man who had a crisis of faith and for a short time he even fell away from the church. Later, in God's plan, he went on to become a priest in the Roman Catholic Church. In time the seed that had been planted by his parents and faith community bore fruit.

Another concern that worries faithful churchgoers is when members of the faith community stop attending services. Good news! They are not lost. As long as the faith community loves these members and prays for them, they are still bound up in God's love in much the same way as a family member is who stops attending family gatherings. As long as the family loves that member, he or she is bound to the family. So we must keep the invitations going out, the door open, and our hearts open. God has an everlasting love for each member of his family.

As parents we may worry about how adequately we pass on the important messages and values. I once read a letter in the Ann Landers column about a parent who was wondering what to give his son for graduation. It was a materialistic decision between a car and other temporal goods. A spiritual person reflected on the situation with sage advice. "Don't worry about what material things you pass on to your child—tell him about sacrifice and the Good News of Christ. The rest is straw." It is important to strike a balance between what our children need and what we can share with them. Storing up an inheritance or temporal treasure for their future is a pleasant thought, but helping them now when they are struggling to get training in post-secondary education is more important. But the greatest treasure we can pass on to our children is not money.

Recently I was reading Acts 3:1–10 where Peter says, "I have no silver or gold, but what I have I give you; in the name of Jesus Christ of Nazareth, stand up and walk." And Peter cured the man. The deeper miracle here is what happened at the spiritual level. Physical cures are great, but there is something more precious than silver or gold being passed on by Peter and John.

How do we pass on spiritual values to our children? One way is through the decisions we make in life and the examples we set. I remember facing a big decision about whether to commit to the lay ministries formation program. Three years of ten weekends a year is a great deal of time. Financial commitment is a consideration as well. One of the deciding factors was how this decision would affect my children. The spiritual training, the work in lay ministry and the example I would set for them added up to an easier decision. The sage advice of my late mother also echoed in my mind: "Whenever you have a decision to make, think of the right and wrong of it, and make your decision for the Lord."

One other consideration I would draw to my reader is the need for peace in the family. Peace begins with loving parents. In a "men are from Mars, women are from Venus" joke, the man says, "She keeps asking me, 'Do you love me?' I told her I loved her when we got married. If anything changes, I will let her know." Being in touch with a loved one is almost as important as our being in touch with God. God is always ready for a new beginning in our relationship. We may mess up, but God is always ready to hear, "I love you, Lord, like I told you when I was baptized." Our personal relationships, especially in the family, should also be a target of our daily attention.

Too much complaining and not enough praising will cast a gloomy atmosphere over a household. Where would you rather spend your life, in an upbeat atmosphere or in one that is constantly over-shadowed by a complainer? In my training to work with a teacher intern there was a great emphasis on always starting a conference with positive achievements, emphasizing the things that worked well. I seldom failed to do this, but when I did, I felt like I was complaining and the conference was not as enjoyable or productive. What would happen to family life if husbands and wives, parents and children always made an effort to bless each other with expressions of love and encouragement? We know what happens when we choose to complain and use our positions of authority or power to make sure the right way will prevail.

Our social and workplace interactions depend on the same principles. We need to care enough not just to work that justice is done, but that a new beginning is made. Enthusiasm and happiness are the result of moving on to a better and more effective way of doing things. For the really difficult situations we will encounter in life, we will need to ask God's help to turn our hearts of stone into hearts of flesh. As we learn from and teach in our situations, let us always look for the fresh sparkle of a new beginning.

One final area I want to explore in this section on family concerns the family of Christ to which we all belong. The concept of the Communion of Saints which we find in mainline Christian faiths talks about a unity among the saints in heaven, the souls in purgatory (those who have died but are not yet worthy of heaven) and the faithful on earth. Sometimes we become more aware of the reality of "other world" members of our families and community.

I recently had a glimpse of heaven. Truly! It was at a family reunion, during a Mass celebrated at the Retreat House in Saskatoon. The family was that of George Rolheiser and Mathilda Gartner, my parents, who looked on from heaven. Two of my sisters, a brother-in-law, a nephew, a father-in-law and many relatives and friends looked on as well. Almost all of George and Mathilda's offspring and their various extended families, some 140 of us, from California to Rome, from Canora to Cactus Lake, even all the members from Klein's province (Alberta), were present. This was the picture. For an hour all the offspring of George and Mathilda's family were gathered in joy, praising God, without even the excuse of a wedding or a funeral. Some looked on from above with even greater joy and vision and praise. It was a gathering of joy, a holiday, a Holy Day.

Some thirty years earlier the late Bishop Mahoney of Saskatoon ordained my brother Ron to the priesthood in Macklin, Saskatchewan. There was a family gathering then, and George and Mathilda were also watching from above. The Bishop thanked my Mom and Dad for the souls they had created in God's Kingdom. His vision was keen. God's will had been clear to my Mother and Father. They had cooperated with God's graces and added sixteen children to God's Kingdom.

I once saw my parents walking hand in hand in the evening of a summer day on our small farm near Cactus Lake. They were looking at the grain fields, as they often did, discussing their dreams and hopes for the future. Their vision made this new century gathering possible. I still see them as clearly as I saw them discussing their financial hardships and the possibility that they might lose the farm. Times were tough. But what life would there be elsewhere for the children? How do you uproot what is your community, your life? Grace prevailed and the Lord provided enough to get by. I made the last payments to the Land Bank the year my Father died.

At the Eucharistic (a word that means "Thanksgiving") gathering the fruits of my parents' love, blessed by God, continued to be in evidence. Infants were chirping like birds in a forest glade. Life was teeming. For a brief moment I glanced ahead fifty years, or a hundred years, to a subsequent Rolheiser reunion, to the Ken and Linda branch. And I wondered how it would be. But I had no fear. Our parents, both Linda's and mine, have showed us the path.

I will conclude this chapter with a brief reflection on the love of our heavenly Father for his family, for us. My question is: How often do we encounter God in an intimate way? I recently experienced just such an encounter. I was preparing a little reflection for an after-Easter lay-presided service when it happened. I had just finished an Easter weekend visit with my children. Part of the weekend involved some one-on-one exchange.

After the weekend I had the realization that if I as a father loved my children in the daily concerns of their lives, that our heavenly Father is concerned about us even in a more perfect way. As parents we pray for our children when they are studying hard or writing exams, having a job interview or starting a new job, under stress or with health concerns, and we even pray for their life choices in careers and marriage partners. I remember sitting with my son on this Easter weekend and discussing some of the above concerns.

I reflected also how as a loving parent I don't dwell on the mistakes my children make, but I rejoice at their efforts and successes. Love sees only the good. Love rejoices at the efforts and struggles to do well. And I thought how our heavenly Father loves us and is always concerned about our efforts and successes.

But it was not until I was in church on Tuesday morning that the reality struck me at a very personal level. God loves me, personally. He is a Father who is in touch with my daily concerns. Suddenly I was choking with emotion. I realized that God was as close to me as I was to my children. And I know God loves all of us in the same way. He is more perfect at this business of love than we as mortals are. All we need to do is to take the time, occasionally, to sit and visit, Father to son, Father to daughter.

I know we have a certain fear as creature to creator. We fear the wrath of God against our human failures. But God spoke about that centuries ago through Isaiah:

> For a brief moment I abandoned you,
>   but with great compassion I will gather you.
> In overflowing wrath for a moment
>   I hid my face from you,
> but with everlasting love I will have compassion
>   on you,
> says the LORD, your Redeemer
>   ...
>   my steadfast love shall not depart from you,
>   and my covenant of peace shall not be removed
>   ...
>   you shall be far from oppression, for you shall
>   not fear;
>   and from terror, for it shall not come near you.
> (Isaiah 54:7–8, 10, 14).

NOTES

[ix] Jack Canfield and Mark Victor Hansen, *A 3rd Serving of Chicken Soup for the Soul* (Deerfield Beach, Fla.: Health Communications, 1996).
[x] Canfield and Hansen, *A 3rd Serving of Chicken Soup for the Soul.*

CHAPTER THIRTEEN

The Afterlife

One of the most definitive and convincing statements about the afterlife comes from Job 19:23–27:

> O that my words were written down!
>   O that they were inscribed in a book!
> O that with an iron pen and with lead
>   they were engraved on a rock forever!

Job is so absolutely certain of the fact that there is an eternal life. He goes on:

> For I know that my Redeemer lives,
>   and that at the last he will stand upon the earth
>   ...
>   in my flesh I shall see God...

Recent events have conspired to impress upon me, once again, that we can be absolutely certain of life after death. When we have doubt, it is because we have forgotten our stories of salvation. We need to visit Scripture daily, and we need to be attuned to the daily workings of God around us. Let me share a couple of examples. A nephew of mine hit a train in the dark of night. His truck was absolutely demolished. His mother emailed me a picture of it. It was hardly recognizable as a truck—pieces were missing and it was crushed like a tin can. One of the clean-up crew asked, "How many people were killed in this collision?"

Several days after the accident, my nephew confided that two men had pulled him from the truck and placed him in the ditch. He did not see their faces. A passing motorist picked him up some time later. There was no trace of the two men. His injuries were superficial—

some facial cuts, loose teeth and bruises. He was back at work within days. I have a feeling my nephew's grandfather played a role in the incident. While grandpa (my father-in-law) was dying, his youngest son was working in a gold mine up north. He recounts how his dad came to visit him the same day of his death. His father was wearing his black, checkered shirt, the same shirt we removed from the hospital when we collected his personal effects.

The leap of faith involved in accepting the above events as true is small indeed. Small compared to witnessing a man risen from the dead, a man walking on water and calming the storm, a man bringing the dead back to life, and the countless miracles then and now. Like Job, we can be absolutely sure of our faith in Jesus Christ and in the Father. Job's pronouncement came in spite of incredible personal suffering. In Job 1:6–22 we read how Satan was allowed to test Job: his oxen and donkeys were carried off and his servants slain; his sheep and servants were consumed by fire; his camels were carried off and the servants killed; and his sons and daughters were killed when the house collapsed on them. Even his health was taken from him. But Job's faith persisted: "The LORD gave and the LORD has taken away; blessed be the LORD...(1:21). I know my Redeemer lives...(19:25)." His words are carved in stone for us.

We all suffer from a natural anxiety about death. Even if our faith is secure, the "undiscover'd country, from whose bourn / no traveller returns" (*Hamlet* III, i, 78). makes us tense. Even Christ, in preparation for his journey into Jerusalem, went up the mountain and was transfigured. In Matthew's Gospel Chapter 17:1–9 Jesus takes Peter, James and John up a high mountain and is transfigured before them. Moses and Elijah appear and the voice of God speaks, "This is my Son, the Beloved; with him I am well pleased; listen to him!" Peter gets so excited he wants to set up three tents; one for Moses, one for Elijah and one for Jesus. This passage excites me because the third tent Peter mentions is for someone still on this earth, Jesus, who for a short time was like you and me. The veil separating us from eternity is lifted for a brief moment and we catch a vision of what it will be like for us when we reach the other side of the veil.

Why did Jesus choose this moment to take his disciples up the mountain and give them a preview of heaven? Jesus had told them recently that he was going to Jerusalem to suffer and be put to death. Now Jesus shows them and us what his humanity would look like once it was transformed in glory. God is showing us that our ultimate goal is not to die, but to live. Jesus' suffering will enable us to partake of the glory prefigured in this vision on the mountain.

Just as the transfiguration gave strength to Jesus for what he was about to endure in Jerusalem, it must give us strength for what we will endure in the short time between now and when we share that eternal glory. Already we have the divine life within us that will never die. We have the whole picture and the whole explanation that Peter, James and John did not yet understand when Jesus was transfigured before them. Our lives should be filled with joy forever more. We perhaps are too concerned about the suffering and death that we must face. Surely we must focus on the vision beyond the veil of tears we experience in this world. At Christ's crucifixion the veil of the temple was torn in two, the veil that symbolized the separation between the eternal and God's people. Let us spend more time on that mountain with Jesus, contemplating the vision that prefigures our reunion with Moses, Elijah, Jesus and our ancestors. Calvary will wait.

Another inspiring angle in pondering the afterlife is a New Age interest in angels. Articles, true stories, fiction and movies are bombarding us. And it is a great thing! It was angels who first exploded the news of our Savior's birth on this planet. In the Angelus, which has been prayed from time immemorial, often at the sound of the village church bell, we recount how "The Angel of the Lord declared unto Mary," how the angel appeared to "the Handmaid of the ᵀ how the mystery of "the incarnation of Christ message of an angel!" On Christmas Eve anc sions we can practically hear the angels sing. ℸ in our society today is unprecedented, especiaₗ married to one or you are from Anaheim. All joₗ popular in fiction and in reality.

As a child I was playing near a deep washout caused by years of spring run-off through a ravine that wound for several miles. The flowing water was irresistible, and I, a child in rubber boots, was perched on a huge rock right at the edge where the water roared into the washout. I slipped and plunged into the water. I was out so quickly I am still not sure how. It is as if a huge hand reached in and pulled me out.

As an adult I make a more credible witness and can relate what happened as my mother lay dying in her hospital bed. All of a sudden she fixed her eyes beyond us in the room, smiled, and radiated such a joy that I knew it was not caused by the presence of my wife and me. My wife had a similar experience when her father was on his deathbed.

Angels have played a significant role in how God has revealed himself to us. Gabriel announced the birth of John the Baptist to Zachary (Luke 1:11–20) and the conception, birth and mission of Jesus to Mary (Luke 1:26–38). The Archangel Michael is known as the protector of the church and the angel who will be there to escort us into heaven at the moment of death. Even Shakespeare was aware of this role of the angels. When Hamlet is dying Horatio says, "...Good night sweet prince, / And flights of angels sing thee to thy rest," (*Hamlet* V, ii, 359–360).

Popular fiction gives us a similar story about the presence of God's angels, especially at the moment of death. In a recent episode of *Touched by an Angel*, a mother is talking to the Angel of Death and says: "Are you some kind of angel? Well you're too late. Why didn't you do something?" He replies, "I did. I took her home. She was never alone."

Another exciting story from Scripture tells how the men flinging Shadrach, Meshach and Abednego into the fiery furnace fell and died from the heat. King Nebuchadnezzar sees four figures in the furnace, walking about, singing and praising God. The fourth was an angel who protected them so that not a hair was scorched, and they did not even smell of smoke (Daniel 1:7).

The reality of angels in our world is reflected in many shared stories. *Angels on Earth*. The *May/June 2001* issue (p. 15) includes the story of a young North Carolina girl named Deb, who tells her grandmother about a dream she had. "Last night I dreamed about grandpa," she says. When Deb relates how she saw grandpa slip into a green robe, her grandmother's eyes fill with tears. "He made it, Deb," she says. "He really made it." Grandma goes on to relate, "One Sunday at church...grandpa saw an angel standing on the altar... at least ten feet tall...wearing the most beautiful green robe... 'When I get to heaven,' he said, 'I want a green robe just like the one that angel was wearing.' "

Even Jesus had angels looking after him. After he endured temptation by the devil, "...angels came and waited on him" (Matthew 4:11). We have Christ's assurance that from infancy on we have angels to look after us: "In heaven their angels continually see the face of my Father in heaven" (Matthew 18:10).

The word *evangelos* is from the Greek word that means "bringing good news." In Latin *evangelium* means "good tidings." The role of angels is significant in our lives. An angel guided Saint Joseph's journey into Egypt. We recognize the role of angels in the physical journeys of our daily lives. Perhaps we need to be more open to the intermediary nature of the angels that go between God and us as we spread the good news in our daily lives.

The flip side of this reflection on angels is perhaps more scary and that is the reality of the devil. Did you hear about the preacher who gave a lecture on devils? Fifteen were present. On a more serious note, if someone said to you, "You could scare the devil," how would you react? Would you check your makeup? Would you look in the mirror? Did you ever think the devil is afraid of you? They say fear of God is the beginning of wisdom, but I say the devil being afraid of you is proof of it! I trust that the devil is afraid of us. I believe that sometimes we scare the hell out of him!

How is this possible? Where do I get such a strange notion? In Matthew 8:28–34 we read of two demoniacs who haunted the tombs in the country of the Gadarenes. They were so fierce that everyone avoided the area. As Jesus approached, they shouted out in fear: "What have you to do with us, Son of God? Have you come to torment us before the time?" And they begged that Jesus would at least let them enter a herd of swine. Jesus said simply, "Go!" And they entered the swine, and the whole herd rushed off the steep bank into the sea and perished.

The devil is as real today as he was in Matthew's story. Many have forgotten about the devil, a reality that must please the evil one. The world God created *is good*—but there are lustful and hurtful desires and addictions that can lead us from the Lord and from doing what is right and holy. Choosing the Lord can help us find the strength to overcome the evil one. But the devil is real. I have heard the testimony of Christian priests who have battled the devil in exorcism. I would be unfaithful to my reader if I did not share this. In one incident a seasoned priest was battling with the devil in a possessed woman. The devil snarled at him, trying to attack him to kill him. There was an invisible line the devil could not cross, though it hurled itself repeatedly at the priest. It takes the special power of Christ through an ordained minister with a sincere heart to combat the devil in this way.

Our belief in the reality of the devil and our fear of evil is reflected in popular fiction such as the 1999 summer movie *The Blair Witch Project* which had some people scared to death. But the topic of dying is almost taboo when it comes to editors. I recall sending an article entitled "The Joy of Dying" to an editor. His response was not flattering: "I felt like putting the article down." He did put the article "down." There is a primal fear of death in all of us. As children we perceive death as something that only happens to others. Death is the ultimate terror in movies like *The Blair Witch Project* where the childhood terror of the witch that could kill you visits the adult world.

There is an upside to admitting our mortality as we mature. I learned a great deal about death and dying from my father. As a child I saw his maturity in dealing with relatives and friends who died in the natural course of time. "Death is like waking up next morning in the another world. It is not the end," he said. Now he, my mother and two sisters in my immediate family have been born to eternal life, and I celebrate that fact. An aunt of mine at eighty-one years said that she was ready to go to the next world. A member of a large family all but one of whom had passed on, she said, "When you reach the point where there is more waiting for you on the other side than in this world, it's time to die." She got her wish and we celebrated.

There is a scriptural basis for our trust that Jesus is the Lord of life and that we really do not need to be scared of death. Beyond Christ's own Resurrection we have consoling stories like that of Jesus raising Lazarus from the dead in John 11–12. Saint John Vianney said that anyone who knows the love of God is feared by the devil almost as much as the devil fears God himself. Why? Those who know God's love walk this earth with confidence and joy. The devil tries to fill us with doubt and fear about God's love. Armed with the love of Jesus in our hearts, we can face anything.

What is our greatest fear? It is probably facing death. That is the devil's final card. Thanks to Jesus, we know that death will be like falling asleep and waking up the next morning in God's kingdom. We will not "cease to be." We have been cleansed of our sins and redeemed by Christ. We are bought and paid for. Nothing can separate us from the love of Christ. The devil's best card has been played and Jesus won the round.

Jesus gave his disciples power over unclean spirits, power to cast out demons. When we invoke Jesus' name, we have power to resist the devil. Jesus will not abandon us to Hades. Today we are the Disciples of Christ. Let the devil beware! In Baptism we received the Holy Spirit and became the Body of Christ. Collectively, we are Christ on earth. Let us walk with confidence and joy in God's Kingdom that surrounds us. The devil is afraid of us! He's not stupid.

But there are thorny realities in our dealing with death that make us quake. Suicide and the death of young persons present particularly disheartening prospects. Suicide is one of the most devastating ways to lose a loved one. But there is a great consolation based on hope and the absolute certainty of God's love for us.

As a child I remember one morning in early May when our next door neighbor's son committed suicide by hanging. I sensed a terrible desolation. The only theological training I had left me with something worse than doubt and fear. My "knowledge" of judgment and eternal punishment left little hope for the soul of a neighbor and an adult that I had looked up to. But my training was deficient and incomplete. I had heard too much about judgment and damnation and not enough about love and redemption.

The story is told of Judgment Day and the great banquet feast. Christ is absent from the feast, so Saint Peter goes looking for him and sees him waiting in a corner of the banquet hall. Peter asks him why he does not join the celebration. Christ answers, "I am waiting for Judas." This is just a story, but it illustrates a truth about the love of Christ for each one of us, in particular the lost. And here we have Christ's word on that love. The Shepherd goes after the one lost sheep until he finds it, and then there is much rejoicing.

A mother of a suicide victim once said that if she could only bring back her child for a moment, she would put her arms around her and hug her and never let her go. This mother is showing love, not judgment. And the great news is that God's love is greater than that of a mother. God's arms are always open to the lost and the victim. Christ came to die for the sinner, not the just.

A young girl, a relative of mine, was lost in a world of drugs and depression. She closed the doors to all who were concerned and could have helped her. In her darkness she took her own life. Where was Christ in this real-life situation? Doors cannot shut out the love of Christ. The Resurrected Christ appeared to the frightened disciples in the upper room. He passed through the doors they had bolted in fear. The same Christ descended into the realm of the dead to open the gates of hell to free us from the hold of death. This young girl who only saw the darkness of life was certainly loved by Christ. It was for victims like her that Christ died and descended into hell. How can we doubt the power of his love to rescue a loved one from the desolation of such a death? Christ will welcome her in the arms of love and never let her go.

To me the most consoling story about Christ's love concerns the thief Dismas who died next to Christ. Our lives probably compare favorably with that of this brigand. The life of a loved one who died through suicide also compares favorably with that of Dismas. Yet Christ told Dismas, "Today you shall be with me in Paradise."

Christ has the power to pass through doors that a suicide victim may inadvertently close. Christ came to die for thieves, for sinners, for us and for suicide victims. I cannot imagine his love would cease for one who is most destitute, helpless and lost. I can imagine his open arms!

The frequent occurrence of and the reality of suicide prompt me to share another example which our Canora community suffered. A young mother who epitomized youth and beauty and motherhood was been taken from us. I cannot think of April (her name) without thinking of spring blossoms and beauty. We all felt a loss at the pain of this separation. To her family and close friends there was a void that could not be filled. There was a desolation, and nothing, seemingly, could minimize that. But there was a consolation in the thought that this was a time to weep. The very sorrow we felt was a tribute to the greatness of April's life. It was a thank you to God for the gift of her life. This time to weep also consoled us with the fact that this time of sorrow would pass, eventually.

There is consolation, even now, in the knowledge that April is in the loving arms of God our Father. In Hosea 2:14–19, the Lord tells us of his love for his people Israel, even though they were unfaithful to him. He says:

> ...I will now allure her,
>   and bring her into the wilderness,
>   and speak tenderly to her
> ...
> And I will take you for my wife forever.

Scripture often compares God's love for us, his people, to the love of a husband for his wife. April has traveled through that wilderness, seemingly lost for a time, but she now is surely in the loving presence of our Father in heaven where every tear is wiped away. We cannot understand God's ways or even the ways of mankind and how we use our free will. But there is a mystery in it that goes beyond human understanding.

I will share another reflection of the mysterious ways of God which it has been my privilege to witness. In my youth, the son of our next door neighbor committed suicide by hanging himself (example mentioned above). I struggled with the absolute despair of this. I did not realize until years later that God used this incident and a couple of other events to lead my younger brother Ron, who was fourteen at the time, to a deeper contemplation of faith. Eventually Ron went into the priesthood and into a writing career that has brought God's love and consolation to many situations as tragic as the one in Canora mentioned above. In *Against an Infinite Horizon* Ron uses the metaphor of the hibiscus flower, an unusually beautiful flower, which blooms for but one day and then is gone forever. The health and beauty of our bodies blooms so briefly, sometimes seemingly unnoticed. But each one of us, like that flower, changes the world forever. God notices and marks the event in the great eternal book.

Without every hibiscus flower that ever gave up its beauty, the world would be slightly less beautiful. The death of a flower reminds us that a day of bloom is infinitely better than an eternity of plastic. And so young people sometimes die. And we look on and cry. We spill real tears, over real life and real beauty that, however transitory, has left a lasting impact on God's creation.

Ultimately, a tragic loss like that of a suicide victim or a young person is a test of faith for us. We eventually try to understand the mystery of the gift of life and the mystery of this particular death. It is not easy, but we must pick up the pieces and go on with our lives. In the big picture, the most important piece has now been put in God's hands. We must accept that and go on from there.

When someone dear to us is born into eternal life it is always hard on us who remain behind. But what makes it better is if we use the occasion to renew our faith and hope. Our departed loved ones are at the heavenly banquet feast which we can only imagine. Recently during the queen's visit to Canada, a banquet was prepared at a posh hotel. Wine made from iced grapes was provided for the small gathering of elite friends and dignitaries. The wine-maker was not invited (it was that exclusive), and he was not paid for his product. It was enough of an honor to have his vineyard selected to provide the wine. Compare this feast to the messianic banquet described in Isaiah 25:6: "...for all peoples a feast of rich food, a feast of well-aged wines, / of rich food filled with marrow, of well-aged wines strained clear." Indeed, God is "stretching out his hands" to all peoples, welcoming us to the eternal feast.

Incredible as it may seem, the king is inviting us to the wedding feast (Isaiah 25). We surely want to go. "What can I possibly wear?" we ask. No fear, the king himself will provide a wedding garment (Matthew 22). Imagine the excitement we would have felt if we had been invited to the queen's banquet during her Canadian visit. We would have told everyone about it. The whole nation would have been excited. CBC Radio interviewed even the iced-wine maker, who was not invited, about his involvement in the royal banquet.

The challenge is for us to make remote preparations for the wedding banquet we are invited to at the end of time. Our excitement should spill over as we tell others about the coming celebration. Imagine, again, that you and your family had been invited to the queen's banquet. Imagine the invitation had said you and your family were invited along with your closest friends. I cannot imagine that you would have forgotten to mention this exciting event to your family members and to those close to you.

I would like to conclude this chapter with a thought about the afterlife. Occasionally we stand on the mountaintop (Matthew 17:1–9) with Peter, James, John and Jesus and enjoy the revelation and vision that is Christ, the beloved savior who will make everything well and because of whom we will never die. Often, though, we are tense about suffering and death around us, the Calvary which seems to drag us down when friends or family members die. But God is waiting for us. In a way death is a win/win situation. Death ends the sickness, pain and suffering of this world, but it is only through death that we are welcomed to the father's banquet table where the Lord will wipe away the tears from every cheek.

I want to share a consoling metaphor entitled "Parable of Immortality" by Henry Van Dyke, which describes the departure of a loved one from this world:

I am standing upon the seashore. A ship spreads her white sails to the morning breeze and starts for the blue ocean. She is an object of beauty and strength, and I stand and watch until at last she hangs like a speck of white cloud just where the sun and sky come down to mingle with each other. Then someone at my side says, "There she goes!"

Gone where? Gone from my sight—that is all. She is just as large in mast and hull and spar as she was when she left my side and just as able to bear her load of living freight to the place of her destination. Her diminished size is in me, not in her. And just at the moment when someone at my side says, "There she goes!" There are other eyes watching her coming and other voices to take up the glad shout, "Here she comes!"

CHAPTER FOURTEEN

Advent and Christmas

I t may seem strange to the reader to come across this chapter heading if you are reading this book outside the Christmas season. I remember attending a healing service where the minister led us in responses that included excerpts from some of our favorite Christmas carols. The emotional attachment to these words and thoughts led us to a much deeper prayer mood. It has always been my contention that there is too much joy in too short a season that we know as Christmas. We should foster the joy these Christmas songs engender at other times of the year, especially when we need an inspiration or spiritual lift.

Childhood memories about Christmas may be the sweetest. The very smells of Christmas food take us back to priceless and spiritual joys. Why shelve this joy for eleven months of the year? A dear friend and brother-in-law of mine told me how he and his brothers stood around their mother's deathbed and sang her into heaven with her favorite spiritual songs. My sister, as she was dying of cancer, listened to a serenity tape of spiritual songs. I would like to hear the most inspiring Easter and Christmas songs if I am ever in that situation of waiting and listening. What better to "waft" the soul on its flight than those themes of hope and salvation?

There are, in fact, significant inspirations we can glean from our Christmas reflection that are most aptly carried with us and applied to our lives during January and the months following. One reflection I picked up from a Christmas past taught me something new about being a Christian. I discovered a Christ who is at home with misfits, drug addicts, runaways and rebelling teens. Christ belongs to them and he went to them first! God sent his son to a world afraid to speak to him. God was so far above us, so unreachable, that man was afraid to approach him. In fact the Jews could not even speak his name. An ordinary Joe (or Ben) could not enter the holy place for fear he would die.

Suddenly Jesus is announced to shepherds, the lowest of creatures who could not hope for salvation because they couldn't even get to the temple for the prescribed worshipping. Suddenly God was approachable as a baby with his arms wrapped about him, a baby who needed to be fed, burped and changed. And Jesus was born of an unwed mother who probably accompanied Joseph to the census so that she wouldn't have to be in her hometown, in shame, giving birth out of wedlock. And why were Joseph and Mary turned away from the inn? Probably because of their appearance and poverty.

That first Christmas was an inconvenience and a hardship for all concerned. Normal life was interrupted when Mary said "Yes" to the Angel. Joseph's life was turned upside down and he ended up fleeing to Egypt as a refugee. Later the family had to live in Palestine to avoid King Herod's son Archelaus' rule.

Being a Christian is an inconvenience! Helping your neighbor, visiting the shut-in, going that extra mile for someone else is an inconvenience. But the Good News is it's catching on! After two thousand years one third of the world is Christian. Even more persons use Christ's name—especially in times of dire stress like after a thumb has been hit by a hammer. You don't hear anyone calling out "Buddha!" or "Mahatma Gandhi!"

Seriously, Jesus today can be found most readily where there is suffering, where there are destitute people, where there are refugees, and where there are sinners. The great news about being a misfit or a sinner is that Jesus loved us first.

A Christmas event that applies so well to our other days of the year lives is the story of a Fourth Magi who sets out to find the Christ Child at Bethlehem. As the days of journeying pass, he lags behind and helps the poor and the needy, sharing some of the bag of jewels he was going to present to Jesus. Finally, he runs out of wealth. Then he meets a poor woman whose son is a slave on a galley ship. His heart is breaking for her desperate plight, so he says that he will take the son's place. He does.

After thirty-three years he is freed and continues his journey. When he reaches Jerusalem, he finds that one of the criminals about to be executed is the king of kings. Worried that he might miss his quest, he meets up with Jesus who says, "Don't worry, you have been serving me all these years. I was hungry and you gave me food, naked and you clothed me, in prison and you visited me." We don't know more about the Fourth Magi, but there really is no mystery about who it is. It could be you or me. We know him/her by many names.

Another story about the joy of giving that is engendered during the Christmas season involves the story of Saint Martin of Tours as a Roman soldier entering a city. A beggar stops him, asking for money. Martin had only his frayed blue coat, so he cut it in half and gave the beggar half. That night Martin has a dream. He sees Jesus standing among the angels wearing half a blue soldier's coat. An angel asks Jesus why he is wearing half a frayed coat. Jesus answers, "Because Martin gave it to me."

Father I. A. Shalla, a former pastor in the Canora area and now enjoying his eternal reward, used to say, "If you do anything good in this world, you take it with you to heaven; but your money, your car, your wealth, they stay here." Jesus says, "...whoever gives even a cup of cold water to one of these little ones, in the name of a disciple— truly I tell you, none of these will lose their reward" (Matthew 10:42).

This passage always fills me with joy at wedding anniversaries of twenty-five or fifty years, or retirements honoring many years of serv- ice. I think of it when I see a housewife or husband who has done so much for the family. Money is not the only treasure we can share. Our time and our abilities are great treasures we can give. God can do much with an open and willing heart. "Those who give alms will enjoy a full life" (Tobit 12:9). Traditionally we think of charity as donating money to various causes like feeding the hungry. There is a much wider application to consider. All the gifts and talents we have, be they singing, speaking, healing, evangelizing, almsgiving, and the list goes on—all of these given or shared with others will elicit the same promise from our Lord.

We need to consider not only the corporal works of mercy: feeding the hungry, giving drink to the thirsty, clothing the naked, sheltering the homeless, visiting the imprisoned or sick and burying the dead; we also need to consider the spiritual works of mercy: instructing the ignorant, counseling the doubtful, comforting the sorrowful, bearing wrongs patiently, forgiving all injuries and praying for the living and the dead. Prayer, in fact, is a good place to start. It may help us discern what particular talents the Lord has given us.

Our existence on earth can be described as an advent, a waiting for the coming of Christ at the end of time. A few Advent thoughts come to mind that I will share with my readers of January, March, June and the month in which you are reading this. I once I attended an evening Mass in the church where a wedding had been celebrated earlier in the day. I was struck by a rich symbolism. Pews were still marked with ribbons, but they were empty. Ironically, they stayed empty during the service. The wedding feast was indeed ready, but the guests were not arriving to fill the benches. Advent is an invitation to fill those pews with our presence, to return to God. Advent may be an empty pew, but a little miracle of Christmas is a full church.

The Lord is calling us, inviting us to the eternal banquet feast which starts in our little faith communities in our little churches on earth. There is an urgency in Christ's invitation that we hear echoed in the New Testament: "I came to bring fire to the earth, and how I wish it were already kindled!" (Luke 12:49). The fire Jesus speaks of here is the fire that will purify and inflame our hearts. It is the fire of his love! Jesus often talked about the harvest being ready, waiting for workers. Having grown up on a farm, I experienced firsthand the urgency we all felt when the weather was dry enough and hot enough that you could smell the dusty wheat. It is a smell that is still fresh in my memory. At the time it engendered a kind of harvest fever. That is the kind of desire that must drive us to the cross as followers of Jesus.

Recently I attended a funeral in a packed church. Death is a reminder so strong that it brings us back to stand around the altar of

Christ. Hundreds stand in solemn silence reflecting on the deep mysteries that have captured the minds of philosophers for thousands of
years. As Thornton Wilder says in *Our Town*, everyone knows that
there is something eternal. We just seem to be always forgetting it.
God wants to get back into our lives. It is not his wish that we seem to
turn to him only as a last resort at the end of our lives.

We are called to charity every day of the year, though it seems we
listen more closely during certain seasons like Advent. Here is an
example of how that season catches our imaginations: in 1992 a letter
was turned over to the Child Protection Services at Port Angeles,
Washington. Police, school officials and social services tried to locate
the child who wrote the following letter:

> *Dear Santa Clas*
> *Please help my mom and dad this Christmas. My dad*
> *is not working anymore. We don't get many food now.*
> *My mom gives us the food she would eat. Please help*
> *my mom and dad.*
> *I want to go to Heven too be with the angels. Can you*
> *bring me to*
> *Heven? My mom and dad would not have to by things*
> *for me no more...*
> *A city man took the lights away. It looks like we don't*
> *live heer no more. We do...*
> *I will not slep. Wen you give my dad a job and some*
> *food too my mom I will go with you and the rain deer.*
> *Merry Christmas too you Mrs Clas too the elfs too.*
> *Thad*

We know about the "giving" side of Christmas. It seems that the food
banks are getting more desperate every year. There are more people
lining up and shelves are running bare. But there are positive signs—
merchants setting up boxes for canned and dry goods in department
stores, and not just at Christmas time. Hunger does not stop for the
other eleven months of the year.

There are Advent stories of hope to bring us joy the year round. The story is told of a young traveler exploring the French Alps in the 1930s. He came upon a vast stretch of barren, desolate land. In the middle of this wasteland stood a bowed old man with a sack of acorns on his back and a long iron pipe in his hand. The old man was using the iron pipe to punch holes in the ground. Then from his sack he would take an acorn and put it in the hole. He said, "I've planted over 100,000 acorns. Maybe only a tenth will grow." He said that his wife and son had died and this was how he spent his final years. Twenty-five years later the traveler returned to the same desolate spot. What he saw amazed him. The land was covered with a beautiful forest, two miles wide and five miles long. Birds were singing, animals were playing and wild flowers perfumed the air.

God does work through us, though we often cannot see the fruits of our sowing. The hope of spreading God's Kingdom depends on our sharing our personal stories of faith with others. Each story is an acorn planted in the forest of faith. We don't know if they will all bear fruit. The sharing is usually done on a one-to-one basis, often in the family circle. It is also called evangelization.

How do we, today, nurture the hope of peace in the war-torn, terrorist-riddled world we live in? The answer is simple. We plant seeds of hope in a desolate wasteland. We pray for peace! We work for peace! We tell our story! We spread God's Kingdom and work toward that day Isaiah spoke of in Chapter 11:9–10: "...the earth will be full of the knowledge of the Lord as the waters cover the sea. On that day the root of Jesse [Christ the Savior] shall stand as a signal to the peoples; the nations shall inquire of him, and his dwelling shall be glorious."

One story I have shared as a post-Christmas thought with my newspaper column readers is "My Window" from Lorraine Code (an Internet source):

> Two men, both seriously ill, occupied the same hospital room. One man was allowed to sit up in his bed for an hour each afternoon to help drain the fluid from his lungs. His bed was next to the room's only

window. The other man had to spend all his time flat on his back. The men talked for hours on end. They spoke of their wives and families, their homes, their jobs, their involvement in the military service, where they had been on vacation. Every afternoon when the man in the bed by the window could sit up, he would pass the time by describing to his roommate all the things he could see outside the window.

The man in the other bed began to live for those one-hour periods where his world would be broadened and enlivened by all the activity and color of the world outside. The window overlooked a park with a lovely lake. Ducks and swans played on the water while children sailed their model boats. Young lovers walked arm in arm amidst flowers of every color and a fine view of the city skyline could be seen in the distance. As the man by the window described all this in exquisite detail, the man on the other side of the room would close his eyes and imagine the picturesque scene.

One warm afternoon the man by the window described a parade passing by. Although the other man couldn't hear the band—he could see it in his mind's eye as the gentleman by the window portrayed it with descriptive words. Days and weeks passed. One morning, the day nurse arrived to bring water for their baths only to find the lifeless body of the man by the window, who had died peacefully in his sleep. She was saddened and called the hospital attendants to take the body away. As soon as it seemed appropriate, the other man asked if he could be moved next to the window. The nurse was happy to make the switch, and after making sure he was comfortable, she left him alone.

Slowly, painfully, he propped himself up on one elbow to take his first look at the real world outside. He strained to slowly turn to look out the window beside the bed. It faced a blank wall. The man asked the nurse what could have compelled his deceased roommate who had described such wonderful things outside this window. The nurse responded that the man was blind and could not even see the wall. She said, "Perhaps he just wanted to encourage you."

I want to share one last story about a man who had been told by an angel that Jesus was going to visit him. As he waited in his shop on Christmas Eve, the afternoon light faded. Once a woman stopped and asked him for directions, which he kindly supplied. A child came into the shop to warm up. A beggar received a crust of bread. Finally, the man grew tired of waiting. In his discouragement he cried out to the angel, "You said Jesus was going to visit me. What happened?" Reappearing, the angel replied, "The Lord was here three times already."

CHAPTER FIFTEEN

Lent and Easter

The best metaphor I can think of to begin this chapter on Lent and Easter combines the hope of Advent with the reality of Lent in our lives. It is by design that the mainline Christian churches have set up a liturgical calendar that begins with Advent, marches through Christmas, then into Lent and Easter. In fact the theme of Easter is picked up on every Sunday throughout the year. The celebration of Sunday as opposed to the Sabbath came about because of the great feast of Christ's Resurrection which occurred on a Sunday. It is most fitting that a book on spirituality includes reflections on the seasons of Lent and Easter. So we begin this chapter with the metaphor of the desert, which is also an Advent metaphor.

The desert has often represented the condition of sin and separation from God in our lives. Abraham and the Israelites of the Exodus story, John the Baptist and even Christ literally spent time in the desert. We still have a real such desert on the earth in the twenty-first century, where human suffering and the absence of hope is howled out in a tragic drama.

During Desert Storm in 1991, the United States left between 300 and 800 tons of depleted uranium-238 from the anti-tank shells and other munitions on the battlefields of Iraq, Kuwait and Saudi Arabia. In an article (*Prairie Messenger*, November 27, 2002) Doctor Helen Caldicott points out that this war was, in effect, a nuclear war. The radiation will remain in the area for 4.5 billion years, the half-life of Uranium-238. There has been an increase of six to twelve times in the incidence of childhood leukemia and cancer and, because of the United Nations and United States sanctions, needed antibiotics, chemotherapy drugs and effective radiation machines are not available.

Where do we find help and consolation in the desert of our hearts? Scripture seems like a correct answer, but even the famous Bible scholar Saint Jerome had a terrible struggle finding the meaning of a passage. After weeks of trying to understand the wisdom of one of Saint Paul's letters to the Romans, Jerome became exasperated. He hurled the sacred text across the room and shouted, "Paul, you don't want to be understood!"

Yet we are children of the light, and we look forward to the eternal promise of a "second birth," some of us more urgently than others. Recently I talked to two of my friends, whom I have known for years, who are in a state of advanced cancer. Another friend I visited today (the day of this writing) has Alzheimer's and is looking at where he is in life's struggle. He would like to go back, to experience the family he can no longer recall. He cannot remember being there for his wife when she died. In his more lucid moments he knows that he is in a time of waiting, an Advent.

Pierre Teilhard de Chardin, who tended toward a lonely realism, addressed the need for hope in our lives. Chardin believed in the New World, the New Kingdom promised by Christ. He was once asked, "Suppose we blow up the world with a nuclear bomb, what happens to your vision then?" "That would set things back some millions of years," he replied, "but this will still come to fruition, not because I say so or because the facts right now indicate that it will, but because God promised it and in the resurrection of Jesus has shown that He is powerful enough to deliver on that promise."

LENT

The story is told of a cyclist who was injured in a collision. He was taken to the nearest hospital, somewhere in Africa. The nun who ran the hospital looked at the unconscious man, his dark skin and his poverty and asked, "Who will pay for his care?" The injured man opened an eye and said, "I have a sister who is a nun." "Oh, she is the bride of Christ," said the nun. "Give him the best care," observed a priest. "His sister's father-in-law will look after everything."

As we ponder the Good News of this story we might note that indeed our Father, Christ's Father, will look after everything. If we could only believe that for once and for all! As I reflect on the theme of Lent as a state in our lives, I am moved to reflect upon a couple of paradoxes of human existence. Our soul is the great consciousness we seem to be unconscious of. Our mortal body, which houses the eternal soul temporarily, seems to lead us to seek life in an earthbound direction. Paradoxically, this earthly physical life is sure to end in the decay of death which the ashes of Ash Wednesday symbolize.

The season of Lent is an opportunity to seek the *wisdom* of the Good News of Christ's Gospel. We can make a conscious choice to use our cerebral powers to reflect on our Spirit-filled lives. This will be a conscious effort to counterbalance our sinful acts and sinful nature, which usually involve little reflection on our part. The best sign of a Spirit-filled life is found in the good works a person does. Every Lent should have a project? Forty days to do what? Over the years I recall some very practical projects I have undertaken. One year I decided I would finish the new home I had built by staining and installing all of the wooden trim and baseboards. You can do a great deal of tedious work in forty days. And work is the form of prayer most readily available to all of us.

For a number of years I have undertaken the task of participating in *The Mystery of the Passion of Christ*, as the Canora players take the play on the road again. I realize other cast members are making a tremendous sacrifice balancing family life and job commitments to make this presentation possible. A recent rehearsal on a Sunday involved eight hours of weekend time. A road trip will use some forty consecutive hours. Last year we had a three-day performance that involved over sixty hours of away time on one weekend. Whatever you choose to do for Lent, the key to a happy Easter lies in repentance. God is only too happy to forgive us when we turn to him and dedicate our lives to him: "I am He who blots out your transgressions for my own sake, and I will not remember your sins" (Isaiah 43:25).

Lent begins with Mardi Gras, the explosion of sexual energy witnessed in New Orleans and other cities around the world on the eve of Ash Wednesday. This wild celebration is a sign of the creative energy our world needs to fire our spirituality. There are some signs today that the eros, the fiery energy that drives our souls may be doing just that, giving our spiritual world a much-needed boost at a time when the institutional church seems to be graying.

The nature of God's energy in us is such that we are restless unless we are moving. Fire is dynamic by its nature. Spirituality is what we do with the fire of God in us. The one thing we cannot do with all that driving force in us is nothing.

Lent must be a time of action for us, a time of turning from our introspective preoccupation with sin and repentance to doing the works of mercy. "Ash Wednesday is really not about sin. It is the beginning of Lent (an Old English word that means 'spring'); it is about turning our heads and hearts toward Easter," says Andrew Britz, editor of the *Prairie Messenger*. Britz goes on to point out how the church has replaced the traditional words, "Remember man that thou art dust and unto dust thou shalt return" with "turn away from your sins and be faithful to the gospel."

The traditional Ash Wednesday message tended to warn us that we would all die someday and on that somber note, we better not sin. "Turn away from your sins and be faithful to the Gospel" gives us a whole new dynamic—"turn away" suggests an act, as does doing the charitable works of the Gospel such as feeding the hungry, giving drink to the thirsty. The former message paralyzes while the latter energizes. "Be faithful to the Gospel" demands action, and can fire our soul's energy in a positive direction.

In another article of the *Prairie Messenger*, Jonathan Luxmoore points out that Germany's Catholic Church lost 200,000 members between 1999 and 2000. Our churches in North America are also struggling with the exodus of churchgoing faithful, but at the same time there are positive signs that God is alive in terms of personal spirituality and good works. Donations to charity are up, Luxmoore points out, even though many do not want to be involved in church organizations. There is a strong individualism in society that has brought about such statistics in the last fifty years, he contends. I suggest that today there is a stronger personal spirituality in those staunch individuals, some of whom do not go to church merely because their parents did. I am not defending their position. On the contrary, Lent is a call to repent for them as well as for us.

The direction Jesus wants us to take during Lent is to repent and believe the Good News. If we follow Jesus, we are more likely to be at the Mardis Gras, eating and drinking with the wrong people, trying to give them a glimpse of the Kingdom of God. The Lord's Death and Resurrection has already redeemed the world. It is time to leave condemning pessimism behind and to move forward with the hope of faith. As Britz puts it, "...the church stands or falls on its ability to make God present in the ordinary lives of ordinary people."

The most exciting aspect of Ash Wednesday that struck me this year is not the reminder of how short physical life is, but how long our existence shall be. When we consider our immortal natures and how with God's grace we can turn from sin toward right action, somber gloom and despair should be replaced by faith and hope. Add love to faith and hope, the love that redeemed the world for all time, and Ash Wednesday should fill us with joy. Think of the next billion years! Only an insignificant part of that time will be filled with our present struggles.

Lent is often synonymous with repentance, a tough order for us. Perhaps it is our pride. The Good News is that God is ready to meet us more than halfway.

Jesus tells us the parable of the Prodigal Son (Luke 15:11–32) where the Father is watching every day and waiting. When he sees the errant son returning, he goes forth to meet him with love and forgiveness. The only one who really loses that day is the fatted calf.

God wants us! He is ready to argue with us about it. In Isaiah 1:18 we read: "Come now, let us argue it out, says the LORD: though your sins are like scarlet, they shall be like snow; though they are red like crimson, they shall become like wool." God wants us to confess our unworthiness and to be forgiven. How do we get to that step in our relationship with God? Jesus said: "Believe in him whom he [God] has sent" (John 6:29). Further, Jesus says: "Very truly, I tell you, anyone who hears my word and believes him who sent me has eternal life, and does not come under judgment, but has passed from death to life" (John 5:24).

Jesus died for our unworthiness, to redeem our nature. If we are ready to accept that, the rest is easy. God is winning the argument. If we hear the Good News and believe it, our path is marked out for us. We will be baptized in the Spirit—simply, we will do good works. We will love! We will turn our lives toward God. We usually require no heroic efforts. We tend to think that we have to be a great saint like Mother Teresa or Saint Francis of Assisi. Over and over again Scripture tells us that a humble, sincere heart pleases God. We must believe the Good News. Forgiveness is a free gift of God, not due to the merit or repentance of the sinner, and not obtained by the sinner except through Christ. Rejoice and believe the Good News!

PASSIONTIDE

As I sit here writing, they are crucifying my Lord! This is an experience that must be lived; it cannot be planned. This year I was looking for a Lenten reflection, but the right one was evading me. I thought of the symbolism of spring and new life and hope. But I wanted more. Then the metaphor that is powerful enough for all presented itself.

As I participate in The Mystery of the Passion of Christ performed by the Canora and district group, I stop looking. I play Judas as forcefully as I can. I shout to have Jesus whipped, to have him crucified. Finally we succeed. As I see the tears flow from Mary's eyes and listen to her say: "Why are you crucifying my son?" I weep with her.

As Judas I have a chance to repent. It is a gift, a catharsis. Lent is a gift, a chance to repent. Collectively we crucify Christ whenever we jeer at someone, or hate and malign. It is then we are crucifying Christ. We sin with the eagerness of gossip.

I look at the audience. Some are weeping. On stage some stand silently at the feet of the dying Jesus. Another gives the verbal witness of the disciple John. Soldiers continue to deride, to ridicule. The Passion Play is a metaphor for life. Lent is a chance to stand at the foot of the cross in silence and in witness.

Lent and Easter

The experience of playing Judas in *The Mystery of the Passion of Christ* has given me much Lenten inspiration. It is a journey of the soul to depict the actions of Judas. I caught the spirit of Judas quite naturally, since I am a sinner for whom Christ died. That role was easy to get into. Repentance is another blessing I get to experience as Judas. I get the chance to weep for my sins. That is what Lent is all about. In so many ways our Lenten journey as the cast of this play is a metaphor for our journey in life. During our long bus trips some pray and others sleep. We share banquets together, laugh and cry together. We work hard and share anxious moments, until the cock crows.

At one of the productions of the Passion Play I was struck by a simple image of seeming insignificance that appeared on stage during the production after the crucifixion scene: a pair of sandals, neatly side by side.

I was struck by the incongruity, that in the chaos of the crucifixion, the mad frenzy of nailing Jesus to the cross, the shouts of the soldiers...there was one contradictory image, sandals standing in order side by side. Imagine the confusion of the riot and the soldiers' activities, the helplessness of the owner of the sandals! And yet there they were, their order surviving.

As I pondered the image, a wealth of significance became apparent. The sandals were empty, waiting to be filled. The application was obvious: "Walk in my shoes!" Jesus is saying, "You are my feet and my hands." The sandals themselves have a story to tell. They are worn, weather-stained. Forensic examination would reveal minute traces of sawdust, expensive and perfumed oil, some salt-water stain, palm resin, and Jerusalem dust.

A further reflection led me to remember other shoes. As children on the farm we saved our new or "good" shoes for Sunday church. As an adult I came across the expression: "There will be no new shoes in heaven." That led me to a deeper reflection on everyday work shoes. We may well be judged on our everyday footsteps in the workaday world rather than on the "Sunday Shoes" we wear once a week.

Sometimes at the death of a great leader, especially in the wars of the past, a horse with an empty saddle would be paraded. The empty sandals are like that riderless saddle. But they are something more. They are an invitation to be filled.

Before I leave this section of our chapter I want to share a Good Friday reflection with my reader. In my fifty-some years of attendance at Easter Services the best Good Friday homily I ever heard was in the form of a true story related by my brother Ron. A young man had just recently broken up with his girlfriend. He had also been fired from his job. He became depressed and decided to kill himself. In his agony, he went for a walk in the late evening. His walk took him across some rough country. He didn't care, but plunged on for hours in the darkness of his soul. Hopelessly lost, he eventually came across an abandoned building. Entering it, he collapsed in exhaustion. When he awakened, he became slowly aware of his surroundings. He was inside an old, abandoned church. Rays of sunlight streamed through a broken window onto the image of the crucified Christ on the cross. In a moment of grace the young man saw his life. Tears began to flow from his eyes. He discovered the grace of redemption that turned his life around. The Lord touched him and healed him.

Your story and my story do not end here. Ultimately, in our lives, the only thing that matters is that we turn to Jesus. Christ on the cross forgave Dismas, the repentant thief, for turning to Him in the last hour. To me, the most consoling words in the Gospel are the words of Christ to Dismas: "Today you shall be with me in paradise."

You and I can probably compare our lives favorably with the life of the brigand Dismas who died on the cross. At times we still distrust God's love and think that we cannot be forgiven for our weaknesses. We have but to turn to the Lord as Dismas did: "Jesus, remember me when you come into your Kingdom." And Jesus will answer us: "This day you shall be with me in Paradise."

EASTER

Easter is a time for Love. The chords of an old symphony play, and once again we experience its movements.

Holy Thursday: In the hot, dry and dusty land of Israel, a traveler in sandals arrives at your door. He enjoys soaking away the aches and pains in a basin of water you send your servant to provide. But Jesus becomes our slave. He stoops to wash our feet. This act is a symbol for his entire life given to serve us, to redeem us, to love us. Jesus gives a more lasting gift, his body and blood to nourish us for eternity.

Good Friday: Jesus endures the terrors of Gethsemane—the acts of betrayal and arrest, the mockery of a trial, the shame of denial, the desolation of death. Jesus gives up everything that is precious to his human condition out of *love* for us, so we can be led to the power and joy of Easter.

Holy Saturday: Holy Saturday readings take us back to our Baptism, the *Word* we first heard from our parents and catechists. Suddenly it makes sense. The Resurrection is the proof that all our tears will be wiped away. Heaven will be opened for us. All the effects of sin will be removed. And the love of Jesus continues with his visit to the disciples in Galilee after his Resurrection. He leaves with them and with us the Holy Spirit. The love between the Father and the Son remains on earth, in us, as we serve one another. We are sons and daughters of God, sisters and brothers of Christ.

Good Friday is indeed "the time for lovers." All is fulfilled; our redemption is accomplished; our sins are atoned; paradise is opened, and it is a time for love, for us to surrender ourselves to His love. Jesus did everything he could for us. It is a love story.

On Holy Saturday we rejoice, not just because it is the night the heavens are opened to us, but because it is the night we too can die. In Baptism we die to the old life of sin and accept the love of Christ. In His tomb mankind is transformed and born again into life that is forever. "God loved the world so much that he gave his only Son, so that everyone who believes in him may not be lost but may have eternal life" (John 3:16). Rejoice and believe the Good News!

And Easter Sunday is the day that holds the most promise. Today we celebrate, and for forty days the church liturgy celebrates with great joy. Everything is *new,* like a lamb frisking in spring. Today we remember those who have gone before us—mom, dad, brother, sister, in-law, grandparent, son or daughter, even infant. Their joy is complete. Like Christ, they served us, suffered and laid down their physical lives. Through them we know the truth of the Resurrection. It is a time of love.

Easter does not end with Easter Sunday. The season of Easter needs to be celebrated for fifty days. I for one am not ready to go back to *ordinary times.*

We should be hyperactive spiritually. We have had a feast of Easter liturgical sweets, like a sugar fix. We should be restless with the Spirit in our lives as we move toward Pentecost, the great celebration of the Spirit.

Restless stirrings of the Spirit should keep us awake. Christ came to light a fire. He was restless to set it ablaze (Luke 12:49). In Acts we read about the actions of the disciples in the early church after the Resurrection. In Acts 3 Peter and John cure a lame man. Peter says, "I have no silver or gold, but what I have I give you; in the name of Jesus Christ of Nazareth, stand up and walk." And the man jumped up and walked, leaping and praising God. We could use enthusiasm like that!

Exciting times continued after Christ rose when he appeared to two disciples going to Emmaus. After journeying with Jesus they finally recognized him in the breaking of the bread (Luke 24). After Jesus vanished they said to each other, "Were not our hearts burning within us while he was talking to us on the road, while he was opening the scriptures to us?" This same Jesus is alive today. We need to look for the miracles in our lives and in our churches. We need to "open the Scriptures." We need to sustain the Easter "high" a little longer.

Our daily journey to the Father should reflect the closeness of Easter. How do we encounter God? While he was still on earth, one of the most exciting encounters Jesus Christ had with God the Father is described in Mark 9:2–10. Jesus took Peter, James and John with him high up a mountain (Tabor) and there appeared to them Elijah and Moses. God the Father, a voice from the cloud, said, "This is my Son, the Beloved; listen to him!"

As I prepared for church services one Sunday, I thought how wonderful it would be if we could encounter God in similar fashion when we attend Mass or Services. Then the truth struck me. We do! There is an encounter. Christ is truly present in several ways, talking to us. He is in the Word we reflect on; he is in the Eucharist we celebrate; and most important, he is present in each of us who make up the Body of Christ on earth.

Like the disciples on Mount Tabor we can truly say, "It is good to be here" at the Sunday worship. We need to imagine in faith that God is saying of us, "This is my daughter, my son, in whom I am well pleased." It is hard for us to accept this because we know we are sinners. But God knows we are saints, too. He judges us on our potential, on the direction we have chosen for our soul's journey. He judges us on the goodness of our hearts in our Lenten Charities.

At the end of our life's journey we picture a loving Christ, a laughing Christ, who welcomes us with open arms into the eternal banquet celebration. Wine is poured. All hunger and thirst are satisfied. The same Christ welcomes us in our Sunday encounters with the faith community. And that, my friends, is the same Christ who longs for a daily encounter with us!